AUSTRALIA

(14) 2.00

LOIN — Strong and muscular.

BREECHING

BRUSH (OF TAIL)
Furnished with good brush.

HINDLEGS
Strong.

STIFLE
Well formed.

HOCK
Well let down.

Title page: Ch. Spectre Rhythm Kingdom owned by Steve Sloane.

Photographers: Mary Bloom, Terry Doriza, Isabelle Francais, Judy Iby, L. Melrose Photographics, Ragaru Kennels, Steve Sloane.

Distributed in the UNITED STATES to the Pet Trade by T.F.H. Publications, Inc., One T.F.H. Plaza, Neptune City, NJ 07753; distributed in the UNITED STATES to the Bookstore and Library Trade by National Book Network, Inc. 4720 Boston Way, Lanham MD 20706; in CANADA to the Pet Trade by H & L Pet Supplies Inc., 27 Kingston Crescent, Kitchener, Ontario N2B 2T6; Rolf C. Hagen Inc., 3225 Sartelon St. Laurent-Montreal Quebec H4R 1E8; in CANADA to the Book Trade by Vanwell Publishing Ltd., 1 Northrup Crescent, St. Catharines, Ontario L2M 6P5 ; in ENGLAND by T.F.H. Publications, PO Box 15, Waterlooville PO7 6BQ; in AUSTRALIA AND THE SOUTH PACIFIC by T.F.H. (Australia), Pty. Ltd., Box 149, Brookvale 2100 N.S.W., Australia; in NEW ZEALAND by Brooklands Aquarium Ltd. 5 McGiven Drive, New Plymouth, RD1 New Zealand; in Japan by T.F.H. Publications, Japan—Jiro Tsuda, 10-12-3 Ohjidai, Sakura, Chiba 285, Japan; in SOUTH AFRICA by Lopis (Pty) Ltd., P.O. Box 39127, Booysens, 2016, Johannesburg, South Africa. Published by T.F.H. Publications, Inc.

MANUFACTURED IN THE
UNITED STATES OF AMERICA
BY T.F.H. PUBLICATIONS, INC.

AUSTRALIAN KELPIE

A COMPLETE AND RELIABLE HANDBOOK

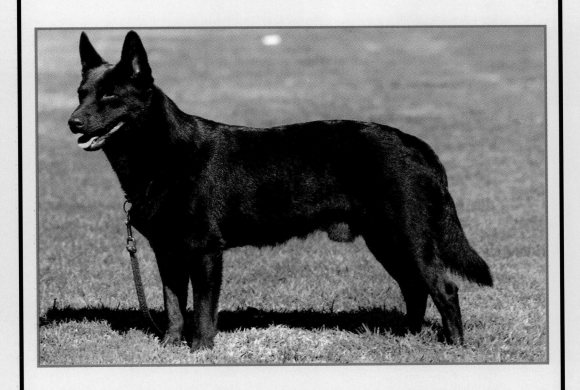

Steve Sloane

RX-130

CONTENTS

INTRODUCTION TO THE AUSTRALIAN KELPIE

The Australian Kelpie is one of the most versatile, functional, and adaptable animals available today. This working dog will impress his master with his tenacity and conviction to work and the loyalty he feels toward his master and his family.

It could be said that the Australian Kelpie is environmentally sound because he is able to adapt to all circumstances and still fulfill whatever requirements he was originally intended to perform.

The owner of the Kelpie can expect years of satisfaction from this dog that is both a workhorse and a friend. If you are prepared to put a little effort into nurturing the natural intelligence and instinctive talents of the Kelpie, the rewards will be immense and will be evident in the satisfaction of you, the owner.

The Australian Kelpie is one of the most versatile, adaptable and hard working breeds in existence. Ch. Oatland Showgirl and Ch. Oatland Pepperina owned by the author.

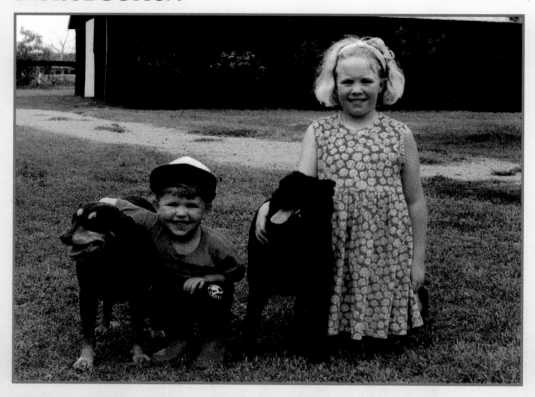

PERSONALITY OF THE AUSTRALIAN KELPIE

The finest characteristic of any breed of dog is his capacity to be faithful. You will have this and more with a Kelpie. If you have ever owned one, you will understand what I mean.

The Kelpie is an extremely friendly and sociable dog whose loyalty to his family knows no bounds.

The Kelpie is a very intelligent, active, and alert dog. Kelpies love their freedom and do not like to be penned or tied up without exercise, but they are quite happy in a backyard. Kelpies are one of the most social breeds in the canine family and love companionship more than food — almost.

Providing he gets adequate attention, the Kelpie does not need hard labor to enjoy life. His greatest happiness is loving care and his greatest disappointment is lack of attention. The Kelpie's expression and personality show off his gay and active nature, but he can exhibit patience and endurance far beyond what we humans would expect.

The Kelpie resents harsh treatment and is unable to concentrate if upset. If the Kelpie is mistreated, he may lose all respect for his owner and will no longer wish to please. Kelpies are very easy to train due to their willingness and eagerness to learn. All these features are characteristic of the breed.

Despite some theories, Kelpies are not shy dogs. They are neither shy nor frightened and they have a gentle nature; they are humble, devoted, and flowing with intelligence.

The Kelpie has an uncanny talent for anticipation— he will often act before you give him the command. His level of common sense rivals that of humans and it is this common sense that characterizes the breed. The ability of the Australian working Kelpie is legendary. He is the backbone of the man on the land. The Kelpie is equally easy to train for obedience, tracking, or show, or simply as a well-mannered pet. You need to have patience and understanding of the Kelpie in order to train him, and you need to explain things to him as you would to an intelligent child.

The Kelpie is a true Aussie. He has spirit and courage to spare. He can also be headstrong, but he is not indomitable; his spirit can be conquered if he is bullied. Destroy the spirit and you will destroy the true Kelpie in him.

Possessing a true Aussie spirit, the Kelpie has courage, determination and intelligence to spare.

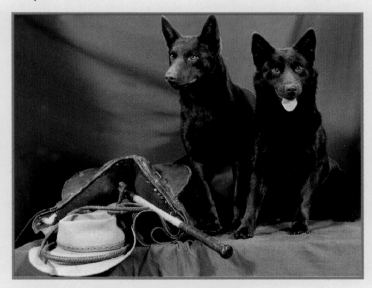

THE ULTIMATE COMPANION

Australian Kelpies are widely admired for their intelligence and working ability, and over the last ten years they have excelled in obedience by gaining top awards all over Australia, New Zealand, Sweden, and, of late, Japan. Kelpies were imported to Japan in the early 1990s for obedience and agility trials and have gained high awards for Sekino Kennels.

In the last three years, a lot of work has been done introducing and training the Kelpie as a therapy pet to work with mentally challenged or disabled people. Again they have come to the forefront, demonstrating good temperament and extreme tolerance of strange surroundings and people.

More recently, Australian Kelpies have been trained with exceptional success as scent dogs as well as for security work as guard dogs, and over the years the Guide Dog Association in Victoria, Australia experimented with Kelpies with some success. They are also widely used in Sweden for track and rescue work, again demonstrating their versatility. Kelpies are only limited by the expectations of people.

Kelpies also have a place as a family pet because they are loyal and faithful to the family they belong to. They love to be with their owners no matter what they are doing; they are eager to please and will look after them to the best of their abilities. Recently, a Kelpie was rewarded for saving his master's life by taking a note pushed through his collar to the first person he could stop along the street, once again proving the resourcefulness and intelligence of this breed.

Opposite: The Australian Kelpie is the perfect example of a true working dog: alert, vigilant and competent in any situation. Ch. Oatland Jackaroo owned by Steve Sloane.

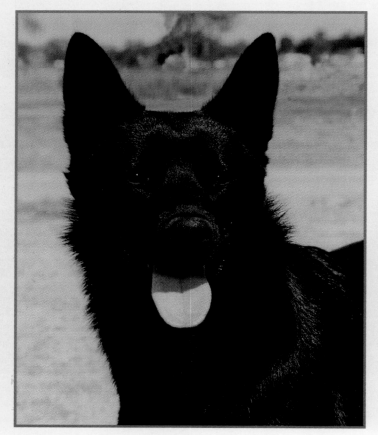

The devoted Kelpie loves to be with his owners and his eagerness to please makes him easily trainable.

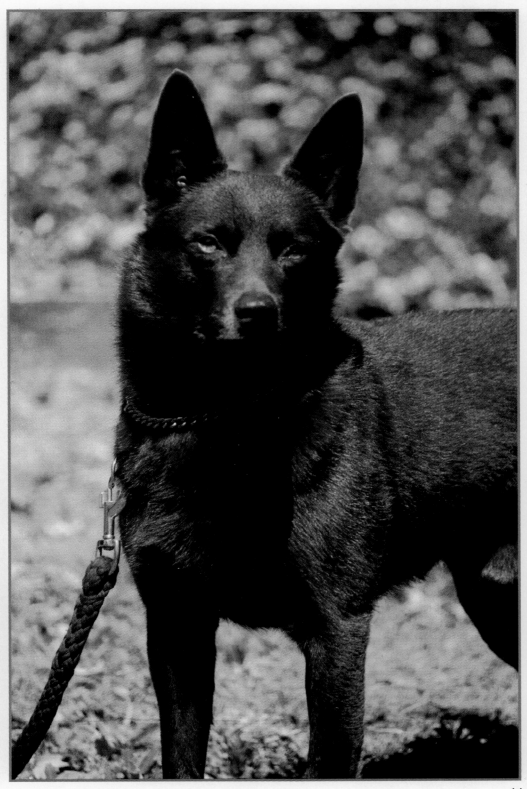

ORIGIN OF THE AUSTRALIAN KELPIE

There are a lot of theories on the origin of the Kelpie and indeed about almost every aspect of the breed. Reading and research on my part has led me to formulate my own theory concerning the origin of the Kelpie. I have also participated in lengthy conversa-

The Australian Kelpie's heritage lies in the rugged, expansive sheep farms of Scotland.

tions with stockmen and senior dog breeders and am now convinced that the Kelpie originated from the smooth-coated, pricked-eared Collie, which was imported from Scotland in the 1860s, apparently to be utilized on the expansive sheep-rearing ranches that developed in colonial Australia.

The first two imported smooth-coated Collies were both of the black-and-tan variety. These dogs were imported by Mr. Elliott and Mr. Allen of Yaralda Station near Forbes in central New South Wales. These dogs produced a black-and-tan pup that was called "Caesar."

The Border Collie, shown here, is said to be an Australian Kelpie ancestor.

It is believed that the Kelpie was originally imported into Australia from Scotland to be used on the sheep-rearing ranches that had developed on the continent.

Mr. Rutherford of Wagga Wagga, in southern New South Wales, also imported a prick-eared Collie from Scotland. This dog was later called "Moss" and was subsequently owned by Mr. Mark Tully, who was a good friend of Mr. Jack Gleeson.

About the same time that Caesar was born, Mr. Jack Gleeson was given a female pup bred by George

Robertson of Warwick Station in Victoria. Jack Gleeson called this pup "Kelpie." The word "Kelpie" is itself a Gaelic word meaning "water sprite." Mr. Gleeson's Kelpie was black and tan in color. Mr. Charles King obtained a female from this mating and she was known as "King's Kelpie." These pups produced black-and-tan pups and a red Kelpie.

At 12 months of age, Kelpie was entered in the first sheepdog trial in 1872, which was held at Forbes, New South Wales. She won this trial with ease. After her sensational trial win, her pups were in great demand and at that time were known as "Kelpie's pups." This was basically the way that this great dog gained his status and title of the Australian Kelpie.

A later mating of the puppies known as "Brutus" and "Jenny" produced a bitch called "Sally." Sally was mated to Moss, the smooth-haired Collie owned by Mark Tully. From this litter a black pup was produced. This pup was given to a part-Aborigine by the name of Jack Davis. He named this pup "Barb," after the horse that won the Melbourne Cup horse race in 1866. This is how the black Kelpies became known as Barbs.

Over the last several years Kelpies have been exported to all areas of the world. Korea, Canada, New Caledonia, New Zealand, Argentina, the United States, Sweden, and Italy all have been recipients of this truly Australian dog.

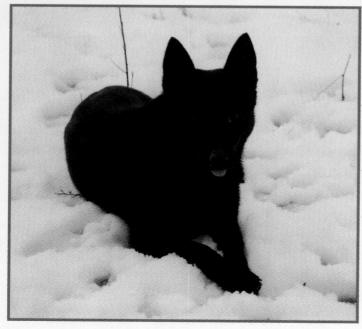

Recently the Kelpie has been exported to different countries and has adapted wonderfully to every kind of terrain and climate. Oatland Briar Rose was exported to New Zealand.

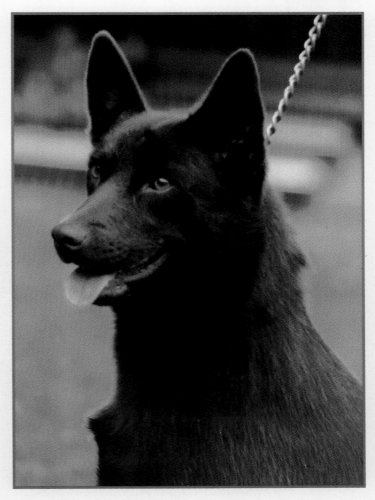

Once known only to the sheep ranchers in the Australian outback, the Kelpie's reputation and demeanor are winning him friends around the world. Ch. Specter Switch In Time owned by Steve Sloane.

All countries to which Kelpies have been exported are finding that in spite of the Kelpie's specific adaptations to Australia's geographical and climatic demands, this dog is still able, by virtue of his intelligence and instinctive skills, to adapt suitably to all terrain, climate, and environment and to work and perform as required, at all levels, anywhere in the world.

THE KELPIE IN THE UNITED STATES

The Australian Kelpie or Barb comes to the United States from "down under" as a much needed and appreciated addition to the world of purebred dogs. This indispensable herder has resided in the AKC Miscellaneous Class since 1941. In the late 1980s, over 800 Kelpies were registered with the organization; the actual number of working dogs is substantially higher.

STANDARD FOR THE AUSTRALIAN KELPIE

AUSTRALIAN STANDARD FOR THE AUSTRALIAN KELPIE

Australian National Kennel Council 1994

F.C.I. Standard No. 293

Country of Origin—Australia

General Appearance—The general appearance shall be that of a lithe, active dog of great quality,

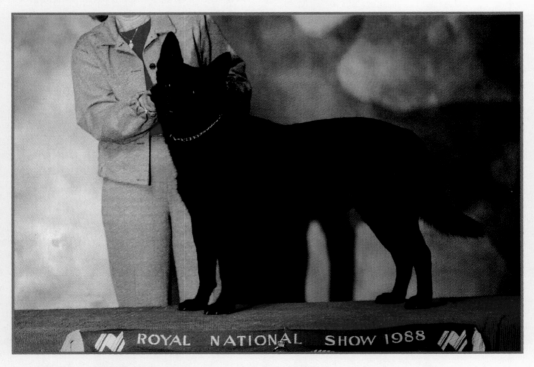

showing hard muscular condition combined with great suppleness of limb and conveying the capability of untiring work. It must be free from any suggestion of weediness.

Ch. Butterbone Keepit Dark owned by Steve Sloane winning Best of Breed at the Royal National Show.

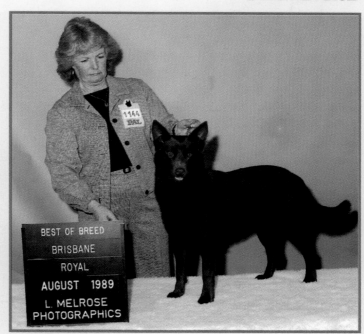

Ch. Spectre Stepping Out, pictured with Mrs. Phyllis Sloane, taking Best of Breed at the Brisbane Royal National Show.

BEST OF BREED
BRISBANE
ROYAL
AUGUST 1989
L. MELROSE
PHOTOGRAPHICS

Characteristics—The Kelpie is extremely alert, eager and highly intelligent, with a mild, tractable disposition and an almost inexhaustible energy, with marked loyalty and devotion to duty. It has a natural instinct and aptitude in the working of sheep, both in open country and in the yard. Any defect of structure or temperament foreign to a working dog must be regarded as uncharacteristic.

Temperament—(See under characteristics)

Head and Skull—The head is in proportion to the size of the dog, the skull slightly rounded, and broad between the ears. The forehead running in a straight profile towards a pronounced stop. The cheeks are neither coarse nor prominent but round to the fore-face, which is cleanly chiselled and defined. The muzzle preferably slightly shorter in length than the skull. Lips tight and clean and free from looseness. The nose colouring conforms to that of the body coat. The overall shape and contours produce a rather fox-like expression, which is softened by the almond-shaped eyes.

Eyes—The eyes are almond shaped, of medium size, clearly defined at the corners, and show an intelligent and eager expression. The colour of the eyes to be brown, harmonising with the colour of the coat. In the case of blue dogs a lighter coloured eye is permissible.

Ears—The ears are pricked and running to a fine point at the tips, the leather fine but strong at the base, set wide apart on the skull and inclining outwards, slightly curved on the outer edge and of moderate size. The inside of the ears is well furnished with hair.

Mouth—The teeth should be sound, strong and evenly spaced, the lower incisors just behind but touching the upper, that is a scissor bite.

Neck—The neck is of moderate length, strong, slightly arched, gradually moulding into the shoulders, free from throatiness and showing a fair amount of ruff.

Forequarters—The shoulders should be clean, muscular, well sloping with the shoulder blades close set at the withers. The upper arm should be at a right angle with the shoulder blade. Elbows neither in nor out. The forelegs should be muscular with strong but refined bone, straight and parallel when viewed from the front. When viewed from the side, the pasterns should show a slight slope to ensure flexibility of movement and the ability to turn quickly.

Body—The ribs are well sprung and the chest must be deep rather than wide, with a firm level topline, strong and well-muscled loins and good depth of flank. The length of the dog from the forechest in a straight line to the buttocks is greater than the height at the withers as 10 is to 9.

Opposite: The Kelpie has pricked upright ears and alert eyes, giving him a keen and intelligent expression. Ch. Oatland Redskin owned by Steve Sloane

A dog must closely resemble the breed standard in order to win in the conformation ring.

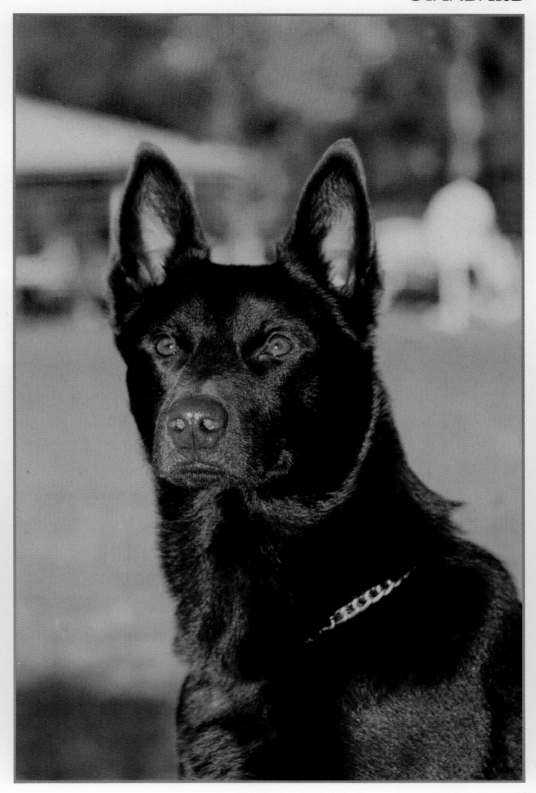

Hindquarters—The hindquarters should show breadth and strength, with the croup rather long and sloping, the stifles well turned and the hocks fairly well let down. When viewed from behind, the hind legs, from the hocks to the feet, are straight and placed parallel, neither close nor too wide apart.

Feet—The feet should be round, strong, deep in pads, with close knit, well arched toes and strong short nails.

Tail—The tail during rest should hang in a very slight curve. During movement or excitement it may be raised, but under no circumstances should the tail

be carried past a vertical line drawn through the root. It should be furnished with a good brush. Set on position to blend with sloping croup, and it should reach approximately to the hock.

To accommodate the amount of stamina and strength needed to work, the Kelpie must be of sound conformation. Ch. Spectre Rimfire owned by the author.

Gait/Movement—To produce the almost limitless stamina demanded of a working sheepdog in wide open spaces the Kelpie must be perfectly sound, both in construction and movement. Any tendency to cow hocks, bow hocks, stiltiness, loose shoulders or restricted movement weaving or plaiting is a serious fault. Movement should be free and tireless and the dog must have the ability to turn suddenly at speed. When trotting the feet tend to come closer together at ground level as speed increases but when the dog comes to rest it stands four square.

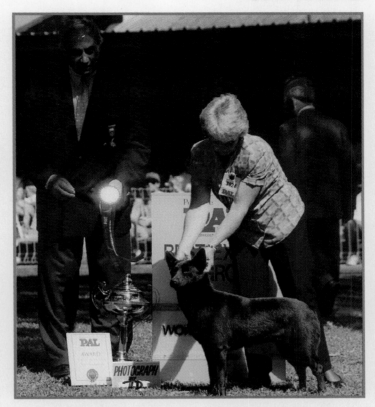

Ch. Spectre Switch In Time owned by Steve Sloane takes a win at the Sydney Royal National Show in 1994.

Coat—The coat is a double coat with a short dense undercoat. The outercoat is close, each hair straight, hard, and lying flat, so that it is rain-resisting. Under the body, to behind the legs, the coat is longer and forms near the thigh a mild form of breeching. On the head (including the inside of the ears), to the front of the legs and feet, the hair is short. Along the neck it is longer and thicker, forming a ruff. The tail should be furnished with a good brush. A coat either too long or too short is a fault. As an average, the hairs on the body should be from 2 to 3 cm (approx. 0.75–1.25 in.) in length.

Colour—Black, black and tan, red, red and tan, fawn, chocolate, and smoke blue.

Size—Height: Dogs 46–51 cm (approx. 18–20 in.) at withers.

Bitches 43–48 cm (approx. 17–19 in.) at withers.

Faults—Any departure from the foregoing points should be considered a fault and the seriousness with which the fault should be regarded should be in exact proportion to its degree.

Note—Male animals should have two apparently normal testicles fully descended into the scrotum.

AKC STANDARD FOR THE AUSTRALIAN KELPIE

General Appearance: Border Collie inheritance in the Kelpie has always been generally accepted despite the fact that earlier in his career he looked more like the Dingo with his rather coarse, fox-like head and long, bushy tail. It would seem that the Dingo played a part in his making especially upon examination of the head with its moderately close-set eyes and under-eye falling away. However, later specimens exhibited a more clean-cut head, still fox-like of course and tapering to a pointed muzzle, but better filled in beneath the eyes.

The Kelpie's skull is slightly domed, and broad between the ears, and the stop is pronounced. The jaws meet in a scissors bite, with any overshotness or undershotness considered a bad fault. The keen, alert expression is very characteristic, the eyes being of average size and

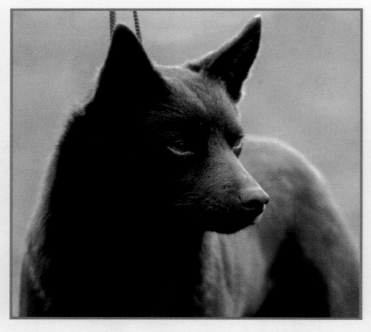

According to the AKC Standard, the Australian Kelpie should have a clean-cut, almost fox-like head tapering to a pointed muzzle.

almond-shaped, while their color may be dark or lighter in accordance with the color of the coat. The ears, which are set wide on the skull, are carried erect and inclined outward, their inside quite hairy. The neck is strong, slightly arched and free from throatiness.

In body the Kelpie is lithe and supple, strong and enduring; he is rather lightly made yet must not approach the Greyhound type. The chest is deep, the back moderately long, and the body as a whole narrow rather than robust, with ribs well sprung but not too rounded.

Shoulders are clean, muscular and sloping, and the rather fine-boned forelegs are straight except for the barely perceptible bend at the pastern joint when viewed from the side.

The hindquarters are notably muscular too, and broad, with hocks well let down and turned neither in nor out since cow hocks are considered among the sheepdog's more serious defects. The feet are round, with close, well arched toes, thick tough pads and heavy nails. When the dog stands at rest the tail hangs down in a slight curve but when moving or under excitement it is raised. It should not however be elevated above the level of its root. Furnished with a good brush, it should reach to the hock joint.

The coat is short, straight and dense, its texture harsh and its color varied; it may be black, black and tan, red, red and tan, fawn, chocolate or smoke blue. Many of the early Kelpies were black, although at that time there were also a few blues as well as an attractive red variety with amber eyes, liver-colored nose and lips, and longer Collie coat. These earlier blacks are said to have been of larger size, whereas the reds, blues and fawns are smaller. The currently accepted height at the withers is from eighteen to twenty inches for dogs and from

The Kelpie's coat should be short, straight and dense, of harsh texture and may be a variety of colors including black, black and tan, red, fawn, chocolate or smoke blue.

Ch. Butterbone Keepit Dark with Steve Sloane winning Best in Show at an Australian Working Dog show in 1989.

seventeen to nineteen inches for bitches, with a body length-to-height proportion as ten is to nine.

Summary: *Head*—Fox-like. Skull broad and slightly domed. Muzzle tapering to a point. Stop pronounced. Scissors bite. Ears set wide, carried erect and inclined outward. Eyes, average in size, almond-shaped; color dark, or lighter to harmonize with color of coat. Expression keen, alert. Neck arched and throat dry.

Body—Rather lightly built and a trifle longer than it is high (10–9). Back moderately long, the chest deep and shoulders sloping. Forelegs straight, rather fine boned and slightly angulated at pastern joints. Hindquarters broad and muscular, hocks well let down and parallel when viewed from behind. Feet round, high-arched, close-toed. Pads thick and nails heavy.

Tail—Reaching to the hock joints. Carried down-curved when at rest, raised in action. Brush.

Coat—Short, straight, dense. Texture harsh.

Color—Black, black and tan, red, red and tan, fawn, chocolate or smoke blue.

Size—Height, dogs average 18 to 20 inches at shoulder, bitches 17 to 19 inches. Weight from 25 to 30 pounds.

Opposite: The Kelpie, once a strictly utilitarian dog, is finally coming into his own in the show ring and gaining an enthusiastic following.

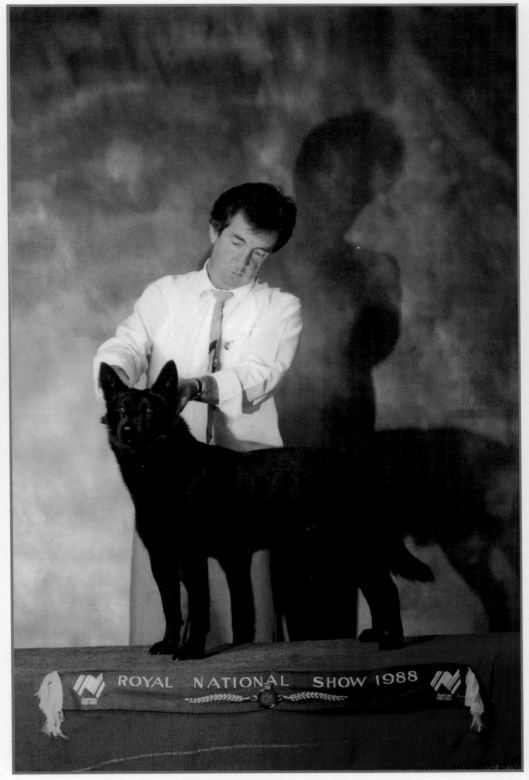

ROYAL NATIONAL SHOW 1988

THE WORKING AUSTRALIAN KELPIE

Australia is a vast country of an extreme hot and cold climate with many millions of sheep, both fat lamb and wool. The very large sheep properties would be hard to manage without the Kelpie. He is considered to be better than six men when it comes to mustering and yard work at shearing time. The Kelpie works tirelessly, sometimes for 12 hours a day in extreme temperatures over 104° Fahrenheit. During winter, when temperatures may drop to freezing, the Kelpie is still a reliable and dependable worker.

With the pressing need for efficiency in the sheep industry today, there exists a justifiable demand for the careful training of the sheepdog, and these days the stockman who becomes proficient in the proper training of these dogs becomes a great asset to the industry. We owe it to ourselves and to the Kelpie to train them in a way that makes for mutual understanding and

The Kelpie has long been an integral and vital part of sheep farming in Australia.

harmony in the efficient control of stock, for it is here that the stockman with well-trained dogs proves his real worth to his employer. Needless harassment of livestock is of course uneconomical, with the weight gains of grazing easily being lost faster then they can be put on. That is where good dogs can save the farmer time, energy, and money.

Generally speaking, no two dogs are identical in their temperament. There is only one constant characteristic in the Kelpie, and that is his instinctive reaction, which is always perfectly logical in situations that confront him.

The Kelpie's behavior is the logical result of previous experiences, or the lack of them. Very often, problems such as the biting of stock, rough careless work, working in too close, and many other faults are due to an overworked or tired dog. Temper and rough work are

There is nothing more economical and valuable to a sheep farmer than a well-trained Australian Kelpie. An adult Kelpie helps train this pup to work sheep.

developed from working too long on tired sheep. The lack of command results in dogs running about on sheep with the dogs not completing the task they were sent to do.

A Kelpie is usually a very steady worker. Very often the Kelpie will move on to his sheep silently and when asked to bark will do so. I firmly believe that a good stockman who keeps fully competent dogs, has them under proper command, and works stock quietly and smoothly does so because of a sense of efficiency.

For the Kelpie's outstanding contribution to the sheep industry, his reward of wholesome food and a warm kennel is, after all, a relatively small return. Through summer heat and dust and the rigors of winter, on the high range or lowlands or on the road, the Kelpie gives his all for little in return.

SHEEPDOG TRIALS

Australia's sheepdog trials go back over a century to when Kelpies were being recognized as a distinctive type of dog. Sheepdog trials are judged on how quickly and efficiently a dog can drive three to seven sheep through a series of gates and pens with only vocal instructions from his master. Sheepdog trials are very popular in Australia, with over 100 dogs being entered in some competitions, now held over a wide area of rural Australia.

Possibly the most renowned Kelpie in sheepdog trial history was a smokey blue dog named "Coil." This dog was the winner of the Sydney Sheepdog Trials in 1898. In the first round of the trial, Coil gained the

maximum number of points. That same evening Coil had an accident, the result being a fractured foreleg. The owner of Coil, John Quinn of Cootamundra, New South Wales, placed the foreleg of the dog in a splint, and the following day Coil competed again. In the second round, Coil covered the course on three legs, again emerging as the champion with another faultless performance.

The Kelpie's inherent drive to work and tractability makes him a natural contender in sheepdog trials and obedience training.

THE KELPIE IN THE SHOW RING

Australian Kelpies do exceptionally well on the show circuit. The Kelpie as a breed was first shown at Sydney Royal in the early 1900s. They attract a lot of attention with their healthy and robust coats, which hold a natural sheen. Over the last few years, Kelpies

The Kelpie requires little preparation for the show ring and does exceptionally well on the show circuit. These Kelpies gait around the ring at the Brisbane National Show.

have been holding their own in Group and Best in Show awards.

Kelpies are not the most popular breed on the show scene, but anyone who has shown and exhibited Kelpies usually keeps on with them as the breed is very eager to please and gives their owners immense pleasure and satisfaction.

The preparation of the Kelpie for the show ring compared to other breeds is very minimal. A good shampooing along with a little homework on getting your dog to gait is all that is needed to begin preparing your Kelpie for the show ring. Kelpies do not need hours of grooming, as is often the case with longhaired dogs. To groom your Kelpie, whether it be for everyday purposes or for the show ring, you will need a comb, brush, nail clippers, a high-quality dog shampoo and conditioner, and a small piece of lamb's wool to heighten the sheen of the coat.

OBEDIENCE AND THE KELPIE

The Kelpie is extremely alert, eager, and highly intelligent. It is obvious that the Kelpie was bred to work in the open country, but many people keep them in their homes as pets and companions. However, people do find that the Kelpie needs an outlet for his inexhaustible energy.

Because of their energy and intelligence, Kelpies adapt very well to obedience work. Another feature of obedience work that is enjoyed by the Kelpie is tracking. In this pursuit, the dog is trained to follow the trail of a person merely from the scent left at the beginning of the track by means of an article of clothing. With sufficient training, it is possible for the dog to find a person by tracking over miles of country.

Over the last few decades, obedience work between dog and man has become very popular. These competitions are run by the many obedience clubs throughout the world that are governed by the canine authorities that control dog show activities.

I would strongly recommend that anyone starting off with a Kelpie as a pet become involved with obedience work. There would be no better way to get to know this highly intelligent breed of dog. Obedience training really would be complementary to the Kelpie, as he was bred for work; therefore, if you don't have the facilities for him to work livestock, his energy in this area can be productively channeled into the exciting and challenging field of obedience.

The versatile Kelpie needs a productive outlet in which to channel his energies, and agility can be equally fun for the dog and handler. This red-and-tan Kelpie wins an agility title in Japan.

YOUR PUPPY'S NEW HOME

Before actually collecting your puppy, it is better that you purchase the basic items you will need in advance of the pup's arrival date. This allows you more opportunity to shop around and ensure you have exactly what you want rather than having to buy lesser quality in a hurry.

It is always better to collect the puppy as early in the day as possible. In most instances this will mean that the puppy has a few hours with your family before it is time to retire for his first night's sleep away from his former home.

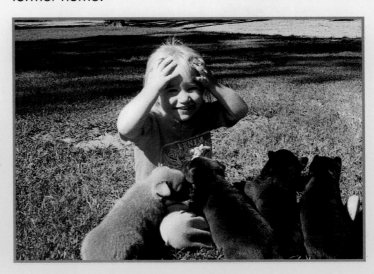

When faced with a selection of adorable Kelpie puppies, how do you choose just one?

If the breeder is local, then you may not need any form of box to place the puppy in when you bring him home. A member of the family can hold the pup in his lap—duly protected by some towels just in case the puppy becomes car sick! Be sure to advise the breeder at what time you hope to arrive for the puppy, as this will obviously influence the feeding of the pup that morning or afternoon. If you arrive early in the day, then they will likely only give the pup a light breakfast so as to reduce the risk of travel sickness.

PUPPY'S NEW HOME

At eight weeks of age, these pups are old enough to leave their breeder. Before bringing a Kelpie into your home, be sure to carefully consider the responsibilities and commitment of dog ownership.

If the trip will be of a few hours duration, you should take a travel crate with you. The crate will provide your pup with a safe place to lie down and rest during the trip. During the trip, the puppy will no doubt wish to relieve his bowels, so you will have to make a few stops. On a long journey you may need a rest yourself, and can take the opportunity to let the puppy get some fresh air. However, do not let the puppy walk where there may have been a lot of other dogs because he might pick up an infection. Also, if he relieves his bowels at such a time, do not just leave the feces where they were dropped. This is the height of irresponsibility. It has resulted in many public parks and other places actually banning dogs. You can purchase poop-scoops from your pet shop and should have them with you whenever you are taking the dog out where he might foul a public place.

When this Kelpie puppy is old enough to leave his mother he will need a reliable and loving owner to provide him with the care he needs.

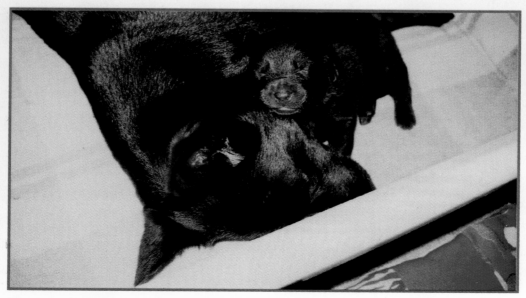

Your journey home should be made as quickly as possible. If it is a hot day, be sure the car interior is amply supplied with fresh air. It should never be too hot or too cold for the puppy. The pup must never be placed where he might be subject to a draft. If the journey requires an overnight stop at a motel, be aware that other guests will not appreciate a puppy crying half the night. You must regard the puppy as a baby and comfort him so he does not cry for long periods. The worst thing you can do is to shout at or smack him. This will mean your relationship is off to a really bad start. You wouldn't smack a baby, and your puppy is still very much just this.

ON ARRIVING HOME

By the time you arrive home the puppy may be very tired, in which case he should be taken to his sleeping area and allowed to rest. Children should not be allowed to interfere with the pup when he is sleeping. If the pup is not tired, he can be allowed to investigate his new home—but always under your close supervision. After a short look around,

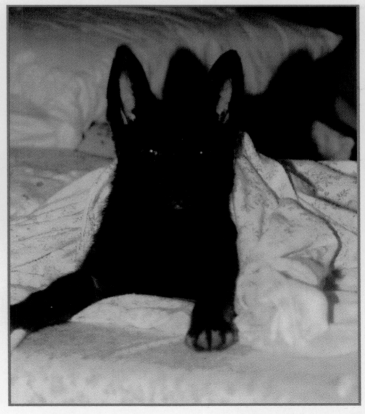

When you first arrive home, give your Kelpie a chance to settle in and become accustom to his new surroundings. This pup looks like he's made himself right at home!

Supervise your puppy at all times when he is outdoors and make sure he doesn't get into anything he shouldn't. Owner, Steve Sloane.

the puppy will no doubt appreciate a light meal and a drink of water. Do not overfeed him at his first meal because he will be in an excited state and more likely to be sick.

Although it is an obvious temptation, you should not invite friends and neighbors around to see the new arrival until he has had at least 48 hours in which to settle down. Indeed, if you can delay this longer then do so, especially if the puppy is not fully vaccinated. At the very least, the visitors might introduce some local bacteria on their clothing that the puppy is not immune to. This aspect is always a risk when a pup has been moved some distance, so the fewer people the pup meets in the first week or so the better.

DANGERS IN THE HOME

Your home holds many potential dangers for a little mischievous puppy, so you must think about these in advance and be sure he is protected from them. The more obvious are as follows:

Open Fires. All open fires should be protected by a mesh screen guard so there is no danger of the pup being burned by spitting pieces of coal or wood.

Electrical Wires. Puppies just love chewing on things, so be sure that all electrical appliances are neatly hidden from view and are not left plugged in when not in use. It is not sufficient simply to turn the plug switch to the off position—pull the plug from the socket.

Open Doors. A door would seem a pretty innocuous object, yet with a strong draft it could kill or injure a puppy easily if it is slammed shut. Always ensure there is no risk of this happening. It is most likely during warm weather when you have windows or outside doors open and a sudden gust of wind blows through.

Balconies. If you live in a high-rise building, obviously the pup must be protected from falling. Be sure he cannot get through any railings on your patio, balcony, or deck.

Ponds and Pools. A garden pond or a swimming pool is a very dangerous place for a little puppy to be near. Be sure it is well screened so there is no risk of the pup falling in. It takes barely a minute for a pup—or a child—to drown.

The Kitchen. While many puppies will be kept in the kitchen, at least while they are toddlers and not able to control their bowel movements, this is a room full of danger—especially while you are cooking. When cooking, keep the puppy in a play pen or in another room where he is safely out of harm's way. Alternatively, if you have a carry box or crate, put him in this so he can still see you but is well protected.

Be aware, when using washing machines, that more than one puppy has clambered in and decided to have a nap and received a wash instead! If you leave the washing machine door open and leave the room for any reason, then be sure to check inside the machine before you close the door and switch on.

You will need to give your Kelpie an occasional bath, but remember to never leave a pup unsupervised near water.

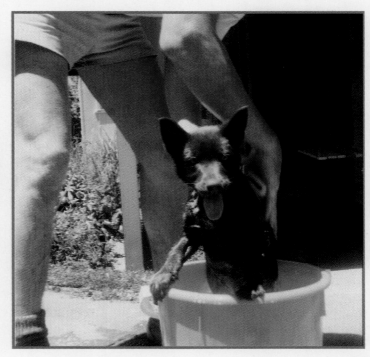

Small Children. Toddlers and small children should never be left unsupervised with puppies. In spite of such advice it is amazing just how many people not only do this but also allow children to pull and maul pups. They should be taught from the outset that a puppy is not a plaything to be dragged about the home—and they should be promptly scolded if they disobey.

Children must be shown how to lift a puppy so it is safe. Failure by you to correctly educate your children about dogs could one day result in their getting a very nasty bite or scratch. When a puppy is lifted, his weight must always be supported. To lift the pup, first place your right hand under his chest. Next, secure the pup by using your left hand to hold his neck. Now you can lift him and bring him close to your chest. Never lift a pup by his ears and, while he can be lifted by the scruff of his neck where the fur is loose, there is no reason ever to do this, so don't.

Beyond the dangers already cited you may be able to think of other ones that are specific to your home—

Puppies love to chew on things, so make sure that all electrical appliances are neatly hidden from view and unplugged when not in use.

Kids and Kelpies get along together wonderfully, but be sure to educate your children about the proper way to handle your new puppy.

steep basement steps or the like. Go around your home and check out all potential problems—you'll be glad you did.

THE FIRST NIGHT

The first few nights a puppy spends away from his mother and littermates are quite traumatic for him. He will feel very lonely, maybe cold, and will certainly miss the heartbeat of his siblings when sleeping. To help overcome his loneliness it may help to place a clock next to his bed—one with a loud tick. This will in some way soothe him, as the clock ticks to a rhythm not dissimilar from a heart beat. A cuddly toy may also help in the first few weeks. A dim nightlight may provide some comfort to the puppy, because his eyes will not yet be fully able to see in the dark. The puppy may want to leave his bed for a drink or to relieve himself.

If the pup does whimper in the night, there are two things you should not do. One is to get up and chastise him, because he will not understand why you are shouting at him; and the other is to rush to comfort him every time he cries because he will quickly realize that if he wants you to come running all he needs to do is to holler loud enough!

PUPPY'S NEW HOME

By all means give your puppy some extra attention on his first night, but after this quickly refrain from so doing. The pup will cry for a while but then settle down and go to sleep. Some pups are, of course, worse than others in this respect, so you must use balanced judgment in the matter. Many owners take their pups to bed with them, and there is certainly nothing wrong with this.

The pup will be no trouble in such cases. However, you should only do this if you intend to let this be a permanent arrangement, otherwise it is hardly fair to the puppy. If you have decided to have two puppies, then they will keep each other company and you will have few problems.

On his first night in his new home, your Kelpie pup may miss the company of his dam and littermates. Pay him extra attention to help him through this lonely time.

OTHER PETS

If you have other pets in the home then the puppy must be introduced to them under careful supervision. Puppies will get on just fine with any other pets— but you must make due allowance for the respective sizes of the pets concerned, and appreciate that your puppy has a rather playful nature. It would be very foolish to leave him with a young rabbit. The pup will want to play and might bite the bunny and get altogether too rough with it. Kittens are more able to defend themselves from overly cheeky pups, who will get a quick scratch if they overstep the mark. The adult cat could obviously give the pup a very bad scratch, though generally cats will jump clear of pups and watch them from a suitable vantage point. Eventually they will meet at ground level where the cat will quickly hiss and box a puppy's ears. The pup will soon learn to respect an adult cat; thereafter they will probably develop into great friends as the pup matures into an adult dog.

HOUSETRAINING

Undoubtedly, the first form of training your puppy will undergo is in respect to his toilet habits. To achieve this you can use either newspaper, or a large litter tray filled with soil or lined with newspaper. A puppy cannot control his bowels until he is a few months old, and not fully until he is an adult. Therefore you must anticipate his needs and be prepared for a few accidents. The prime times a pup will urinate and defecate are shortly after he wakes up from a sleep, shortly after he has eaten, and after he has been playing awhile. He will usually whimper and start searching the room for a suitable place. You must quickly pick him up and place him on the newspaper or in the litter tray. Hold him in position gently but firmly. He might jump out of the box without doing anything on the first one or two occasions, but if you simply repeat the procedure every time you think he wants to relieve himself then eventually he will get the message.

Spectre Begga Dingo at eight weeks old.

When he does defecate as required, give him plenty of praise, telling him what a good puppy he is. The litter tray or newspaper must, of course, be cleaned or replaced after each use—puppies do not like using a dirty toilet any more than you do. The pup's toilet can be placed near the kitchen door and as he gets older the tray can be placed outside while the door is open. The pup will then start to use it while he is outside. From that time on, it is easy to get the pup to use a given area of the yard.

Many breeders recommend the popular alternative of crate training. Upon bringing the pup home, introduce him to his crate. The open wire crate is the best choice, placed in a restricted, draft-free area of the home. Put the pup's Nylabone® and other favorite

Opposite: The Australian Kelpie is a loyal family pet and a natural babysitter. Owner, Steve Sloane.

toys in the crate along with a wool blanket or other suitable bedding. The puppy's natural cleanliness instincts prohibit him from soiling in the place where he sleeps, his crate. The puppy should be allowed to go in and out of the open crate during the day, but he should sleep in the crate at the night and at other intervals during the day. Whenever the pup is taken out of his crate, he should be brought outside (or to his newspapers) to do his business. Never use the crate as a place of punishment. You will see how quickly your pup takes to his crate, considering it as his own safe haven from the big world around him.

Crate training is an excellent way to housebreak your puppy because dogs do not like to soil where they eat and sleep. You can choose between a wire or fiberglass crate.

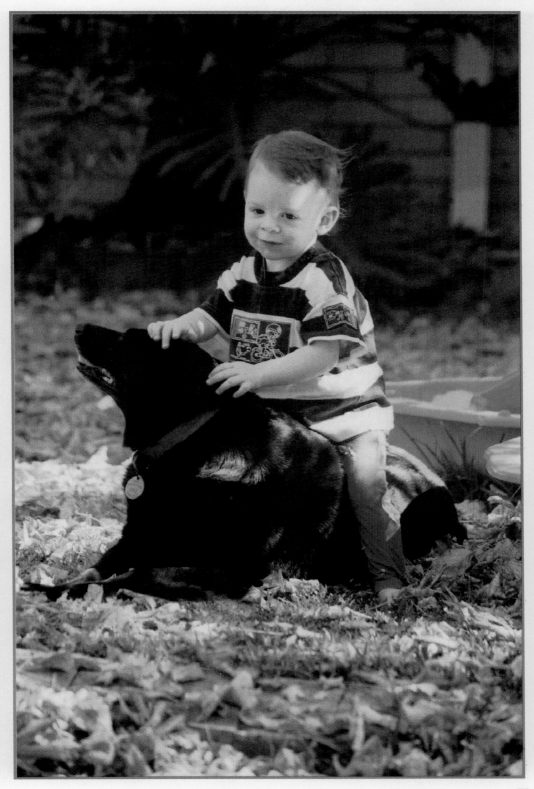

THE EARLY DAYS

You will no doubt be given much advice on how to bring up your puppy. This will come from dog-owning friends, neighbors, and through articles and books you may read on the subject. Some of the advice will be sound, some will be nothing short of rubbish. What you should do above all else is to keep an open mind and let common sense prevail over prejudice and

worn-out ideas that have been handed down over the centuries. There is no one way that is superior to all others, no more than there is no one dog that is exactly a replica of another. Each is an individual and must always be regarded as such.

A dog never becomes disobedient, unruly, or a menace to society without the full consent of his owner. Your puppy may have many limitations, but the singular biggest limitation he is confronted with in so many instances is his owner's inability to understand his needs and how to cope with them.

After being properly vaccinated, your Kelpie puppy should be socialized with as many different kinds of people and animals as possible. This pup meets his future charges for the first time.

IDENTIFICATION

It is a sad reflection on our society that the number of dogs and cats stolen every year runs into many

Australian Kelpie puppies are innately curious and can often get into trouble unless they are closely supervised.

thousands. To these can be added the number that get lost. If you do not want your cherished pet to be lost or stolen, then you should see that he is carrying a permanent identification number, as well as a temporary tag on his collar.

Permanent markings come in the form of tattoos placed either inside the pup's ear flap, or on the inner side of a pup's upper rear leg. The number given is then recorded with one of the national registration

The newest method of identification is the microchip, a computer chip that is no bigger than a grain of rice, that is injected into the dog's skin

companies. Research laboratories will not purchase dogs carrying numbers as they realize these are clearly someone's pet, and not abandoned animals. As a result, thieves will normally abandon dogs so marked and this at least gives the dog a chance to be taken to the police or the dog pound, when the number can be traced and the dog reunited with its family. The only problem with this method at this time is that there are a number of registration bodies, so it is not always apparent which one the dog is registered with (as you provide the actual number). However, each registration body is aware of his competitors and will normally be happy to supply their addresses. Those holding the dog can check out which one you are with. It is not a perfect system, but until such is developed it's the best available.

A temporary tag takes the form of a metal or plastic disk large enough for you to place the dog's name and your phone number on it—maybe even your address as well. In virtually all places you will be required to obtain a license for your puppy. This may not become applicable until the pup is six months old, but it might apply regardless of his age. Much depends upon the state within a country, or the country itself, so check with your veterinarian if the breeder has not already advised you on this.

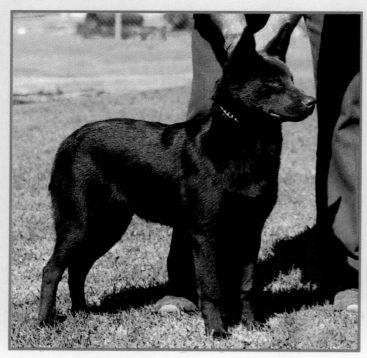

There are many things that can distract your dog when he is outside. Make sure your Kelpie always wears a collar and identification tags in case he becomes separated from you.

FEEDING YOUR AUSTRALIAN KELPIE

Dog owners today are fortunate in that they live in an age when considerable cash has been invested in the study of canine nutritional requirements. This means dog food manufacturers are very concerned about ensuring that their foods are of the best

Kelpie pups get their first nutrition from their mother, and then the breeder should start them on a good-quality commercial diet.

quality. The result of all of their studies, apart from the food itself, is that dog owners are bombarded with advertisements telling them why they must purchase a given brand. The number of products available to you is unlimited, so it is hardly surprising to find that dogs in general suffer from obesity and an excess of vitamins, rather than the reverse. Be sure to feed age-appropriate food—puppy food up to one year of

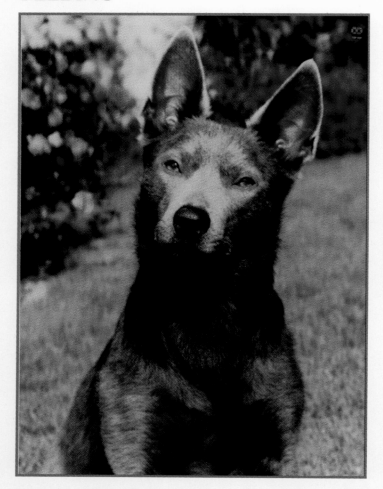

What you feed your Kelpie will depend on his age and activity level. This older Kelpie, Oatland Kirrabelle, will need a diet specially formulated for the senior dog.

age, adult food thereafter. Generally breeders recommend dry food supplemented by canned, if needed.

FACTORS AFFECTING NUTRITIONAL NEEDS

Activity Level. A dog that lives in a country environment and is able to exercise for long periods of the day will need more food than the same breed of dog living in an apartment and given little exercise.

Quality of the Food. Obviously the quality of food will affect the quantity required by a puppy. If the nutritional content of a food is low then the puppy will need more of it than if a better quality food was fed.

Balance of Nutrients and Vitamins. Feeding a puppy the correct balance of nutrients is not easy because the average person is not able to measure out ratios of one to another, so it is a case of trying to see that nothing is in excess. However, only tests, or your veterinarian, can be the source of reliable advice.

Genetic and Biological Variation. Apart from all of the other considerations, it should be remembered that each puppy is an individual. His genetic make-up will influence not only his physical characteristics but also his metabolic efficiency. This being so, two pups from the same litter can vary quite a bit in the amount of food they need to perform the same function under the same conditions. If you consider the potential combinations of all of these factors then you will see that pups of a given breed could vary quite a bit in the amount of food they will need. Before discussing feeding quantities it is valuable to know at least a little about the composition of food and its role in the body.

COMPOSITION AND ROLE OF FOOD

The main ingredients of food are protein, fats, and carbohydrates, each of which is needed in relatively large quantities when compared to the other needs of vitamins and minerals. The other vital ingredient of food is, of course, water. Although all foods obviously contain some of the basic ingredients needed for an animal to survive, they do not all contain the ingredients in the needed ratios or type. For example, there are many forms

POPpups™ are 100% edible and enhanced with dog-friendly ingredients like liver, cheese, spinach, chicken, carrots, or potatoes. They contain no salt, sugar, alcohol, plastic or preservatives. You can even microwave a POPpup™ to turn into a huge crackly treat.

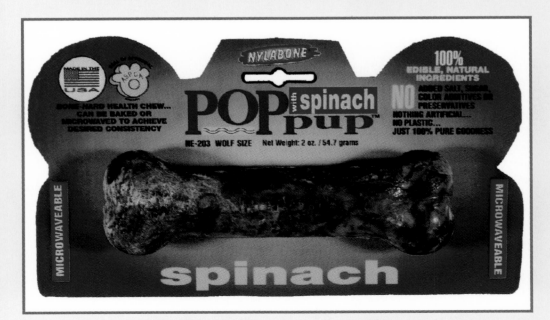

of protein, just as there are many types of carbohydrates. Both of these compounds are found in meat and in vegetable matter—but not all of those that are needed will be in one particular meat or vegetable. Plants, especially, do not contain certain amino acids that are required for the synthesis of certain proteins needed by dogs.

Likewise, vitamins are found in meats and vegetable matter, but vegetables are a richer source of most. Meat contains very little carbohydrates. Some

vitamins can be synthesized by the dog, so do not need to be supplied via the food. Dogs are carnivores and this means their digestive tract has evolved to need a high quantity of meat as compared to humans. The digestive system of carnivores is unable to break down the tough cellulose walls of plant matter, but it is easily able to assimilate proteins from meat.

In order to gain its needed vegetable matter in a form that it can cope with, the carnivore eats all of its prey. This includes the partly digested food within the stomach. In commercially prepared foods, the cellulose is broken down by cooking. During this process the vitamin content is either greatly reduced or lost altogether. The manufacturer therefore adds vitamins once the heat process has been

Carrots are rich in fiber, carbohydrates, and vitamin A. The Carrot Bone™ by Nylabone® is a durable chew containing no plastics or artificial ingredients and it can be served as-is, in a bone-hard form, or microwaved to a biscuit consistency.

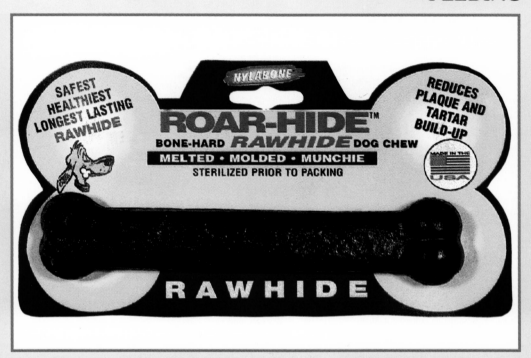

NYLABONE

ROAR-HIDE™
BONE-HARD *RAWHIDE* DOG CHEW
MELTED • MOLDED • MUNCHIE
STERILIZED PRIOR TO PACKING

SAFEST HEALTHIEST LONGEST LASTING RAWHIDE

REDUCES PLAQUE AND TARTAR BUILD-UP

MADE IN THE USA

R A W H I D E

Roar-Hide® is completely edible and is high in protein (over 86%) and low in fat (less than one-third of 1%). Unlike common rawhide, it is safer, less messy, and more fun.

completed. This is why commercial foods are so useful as part of a feeding regimen, providing they are of good quality and from a company that has prepared the foods very carefully.

Proteins

These are made from amino acids, of which at least ten are essential if a puppy is to maintain healthy growth. Proteins provide the building blocks for the puppy's body. The richest sources are meat, fish and poultry, together with their by-products. The latter will include milk, cheese, yogurt, fishmeal, and eggs. Vegetable matter that has a high protein content includes soy beans, together with numerous corn and other plant extracts that have been dehydrated. The actual protein content needed in the diet will be determined both by the activity level of the dog and his age. The total protein need will also be influenced by the digestibility factor of the food given.

Fats

These serve numerous roles in the puppy's body. They provide insulation against the cold, and help buffer the organs from knocks and general activity shocks. They provide the richest source of energy, and reserves of this, and they are vital in the transport of vitamins and other nutrients, via the blood, to all other organs. Finally, it is the fat content within a diet that gives it palatability. It is important that the fat content of a diet should not be excessive. This is because the high energy content of fats (more than twice that of protein or carbohydrate) will increase the overall energy content of the diet. The puppy will adjust its food intake to that of its energy needs, which are obviously more easily met in a high-energy diet. This will mean that while the fats are providing the energy needs of the puppy, the over-all diet may not be providing its protein, vitamin, and mineral needs, so signs of protein deficiency will become apparent. Rich sources of fats are meat, their byproducts (butter, milk), and vegetable oils, such as safflower, olive, corn or soy bean.

Carbohydrates

These are the principal energy compounds given to puppies and adult dogs. Their inclusion within most commercial brand dog foods is for cost, rather than dietary needs. These compounds are more commonly known as sugars, and they are seen in simple or complex compounds of carbon, hydrogen, and oxygen. One of the simple sugars is called glucose, and it is vital to many metabolic processes. When large chains of glucose are created, they form compound sugars. One

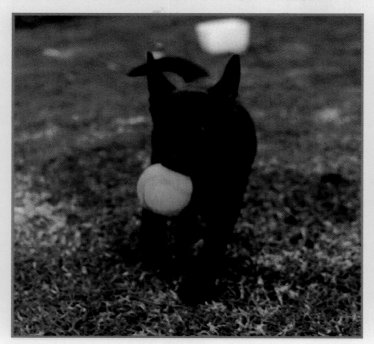

Kelpie puppies are full of boundless energy and will need a diet that will accommodate their level of activity and promote growth.

of these is called glycogen, and it is found in the cells of animals. Another, called starch, is the material that is found in the cells of plants.

Vitamins

These are not foods as such but chemical compounds that assist in all aspects of an animal's life. They help in so many ways that to attempt to describe these effectively would require a chapter in itself. Fruits are a rich source of vitamins, as is the liver of most animals. Many vitamins are unstable and easily destroyed by light, heat, moisture, or rancidity. An excess of vitamins, especially A and D, has been proven to be very harmful. Provided a puppy is receiving a balanced diet, it is most

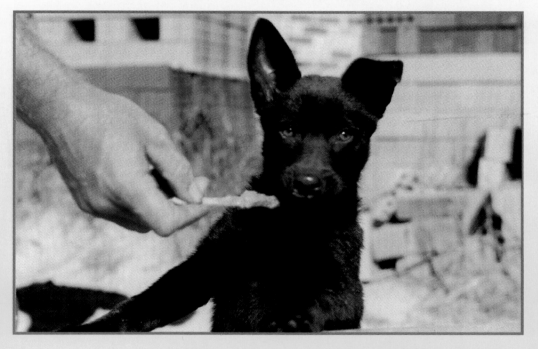

There's nothing like a cool treat on a hot summer day! Ten-week-old Spectre Rythym Lady, owned by Steve Sloane.

unlikely there will be a deficiency, whereas hypervitaminosis (an excess of vitamins) has become quite common due to owners and breeders feeding unneeded supplements. The only time you should feed extra vitamins to your puppy is if your veterinarian advises you to.

Minerals

These provide strength to bone and cell tissue, as well as assist in many metabolic processes. Examples are calcium, phosphorous, copper, iron, magnesium, selenium, potassium, zinc, and sodium. The recommended amounts of all minerals in the diet has not been fully established. Calcium and phosphorous are known to be important, especially to puppies. They help in forming strong bone. As with vitamins, a mineral deficiency is most unlikely in pups given a good and varied diet. Again, an excess can create problems—this applying equally to calcium.

Treat your Kelpies like the valued family members they are by providing them with a quality dog food and plenty of exercise.

Water

This is the most important of all nutrients, as is easily shown by the fact that the adult dog is made up of about 60 percent water, the puppy containing an even higher percentage. Dogs must retain a water balance, which means that the total intake should be balanced by the total output. The intake comes either by direct input (the tap or its equivalent), plus water released when food is oxidized, known as metabolic water (remember that all foods contain the elements hydrogen and oxygen that recombine in the body to create water). A dog without adequate water will lose condition more rapidly than one depleted of food, a fact common to most animal species.

AMOUNT TO FEED

The best way to determine dietary requirements is by observing the puppy's general health and physical appearance. If he is well covered with flesh, shows good bone development and muscle, and is an active alert puppy, then his diet is fine. A puppy will consume about twice as much as an adult (of the same breed). You should ask the breeder of your puppy to show you the amounts fed to their pups and this will be a good starting point.

The puppy should eat his meal in about five to seven minutes. Any leftover food can be discarded or placed into the refrigerator until the next meal (but be sure it is thawed fully if your fridge is very cold).

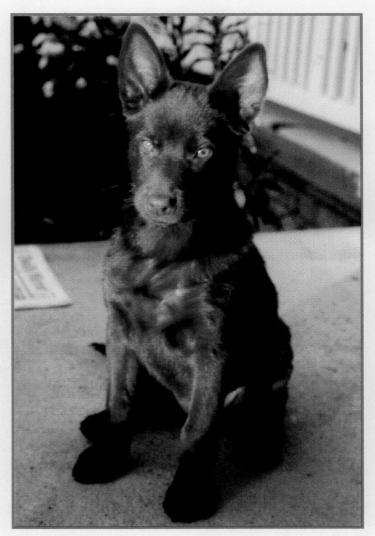

Your Kelpie puppy will look to you, his owner, to provide him with the nutrition he needs to grow up strong and healthy.

FEEDING

If the puppy quickly devours its meal and is clearly still hungry, then you are not giving him enough food. If he eats readily but then begins to pick at it, or walks away leaving a quantity, then you are probably giving him too much food. Adjust this at the next meal and you will quickly begin to appreciate what the correct amount is. If, over a number of weeks, the pup starts to look fat, then he is obviously overeating; the reverse is true if he starts to look thin compared with others of the same breed.

Opposite: Your Kelpie's well-balanced diet will be evident in his shiny coat, bright eyes and overall healthy appearance. Owner, Steve Sloane.

WHEN TO FEED

It really does not matter what times of the day the puppy is fed, as long as he receives the needed quantity of food. Puppies from 8 weeks to 12 or 16 weeks need 3 or 4 meals a day. Older puppies and

adult dogs should be fed twice a day. What is most important is that the feeding times are reasonably regular. They can be tailored to fit in with your own timetable—for example, 7 a.m. and 6 p.m. The dog will then expect his meals at these times each day. Keeping regular feeding times and feeding set amounts will help you monitor your puppy's or dog's health. If a dog that's normally enthusiastic about mealtimes and eats readily suddenly shows a lack of interest in food, you'll know something's not right.

A lake or pond may look inviting to a thirsty Kelpie, but it may not be safe to drink. Bring along clean water from home when you take your dog on an outing.

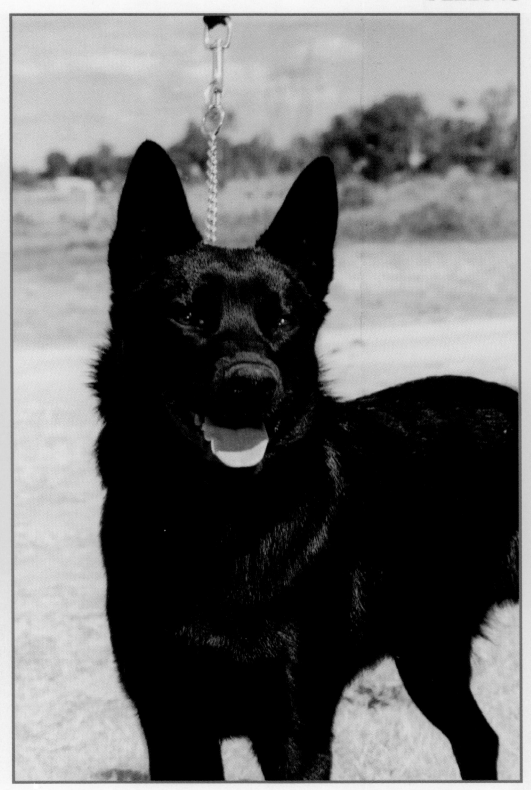

TRAINING YOUR AUSTRALIAN KELPIE

Once your puppy has settled into your home and responds to his name, then you can begin his basic training. Before giving advice on how you should go about doing this, two important points should be made. You should train the puppy in isolation of any potential distractions, and you should keep all lessons very short. It is essential that you have the full attention of your puppy. This is not possible if there are other people about, or televisions and radios on, or other pets in the vicinity. Even when the pup has become a young adult, the maximum time you should allocate to a lesson is about 20 minutes. However,

Introducing your puppy to a collar and leash is one of the first steps in training your Australian Kelpie. Four-month-old Firefox Chloe tries on her collar.

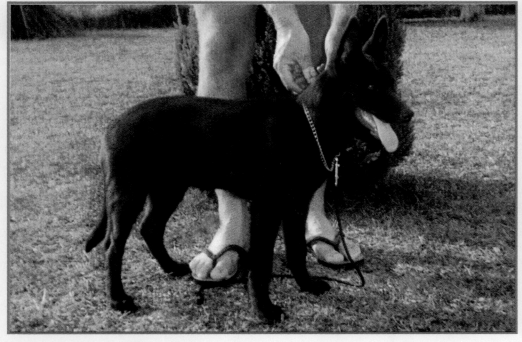

you can give the puppy more than one lesson a day, three being as many as are recommended, each well spaced apart.

Before beginning a lesson, always play a little game with the puppy so he is in an active state of mind and thus more receptive to the matter at hand. Likewise, always end a lesson with fun-time for the pup, and always—this is most important—end on a high note, praising the puppy. Let the lesson end when the pup has done as you require so he receives lots of fuss. This will really build his confidence.

Keep training lessons with your pups fun and always end a session with some play time. Phyllis Sloane with three Kelpie puppies.

COLLAR AND LEASH TRAINING

Training a puppy to his collar and leash is very easy. Place a collar on the puppy and, although he will initially try to bite at it, he will soon forget it, the more so if you play with him. You can leave the collar on for a few hours. Some people leave their dogs' collars on all of the time, others only when they are taking the dog out. If it is to be left on, purchase a narrow or round one so it does not mark the fur.

Once the puppy ignores his collar, then you can attach the leash to it and let the puppy pull this along behind it for a few minutes. However, if the pup starts to chew at the leash, simply hold the leash but keep it slack and let the pup go where he wants. The idea is to let him get the feel of the leash, but not get in the habit of chewing it. Repeat this a couple of times a day

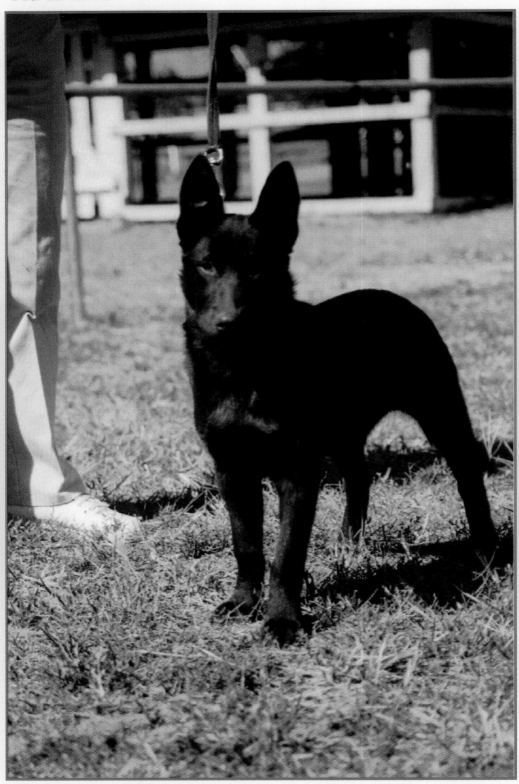

for two days and the pup will get used to the leash without thinking that it will restrain him—which you will not have attempted to do yet.

Next, you can let the pup understand that the leash will restrict his movements. The first time he realizes this, he will pull and buck or just sit down. Immediately call the pup to you and give him lots of fuss. Never tug on the leash so the puppy is dragged along the floor, as this simply implants a negative thought in his mind.

Opposite: It is important that your Kelpie wear his collar and leash at all times, for his safety and for the safety of others.

THE COME COMMAND

Come is the most vital of all commands and especially so for the independently minded dog. To teach the puppy to come, let him reach the end of a long

Australian Kelpie puppies start their training for the herd at an early age. These pups are becoming acquainted with the sheep they are watching.

lead, then give the command and his name, gently pulling him toward you at the same time. As soon as he associates the word come with the action of moving toward you, pull only when he does not respond immediately. As he starts to come, move back to make him learn that he must come from a distance as well as when he is close to you. Soon you may be able to practice without a leash, but if he is slow to come or notably disobedient, go to him and pull him toward you, repeating the command. Never scold a dog during this exercise—or any other exercise. Remember the trick is that the puppy must want to come to you. For the very independent dog, hand signals may work better than verbal commands.

THE SIT COMMAND

As with most basic commands, your puppy will learn this one in just a few lessons. You can give the puppy two lessons a day on the sit command but he will make just as much progress with one 15-minute lesson each day. Some trainers will advise you that you should not proceed to other commands until the previous one has been learned really well. However, a bright young pup is quite capable of handling more than one command per lesson, and certainly per day. Indeed, as time progresses, you will be going through each command as a matter of routine before a new one is attempted. This is so the puppy always starts, as well as ends, a lesson on a high note, having successfully completed something.

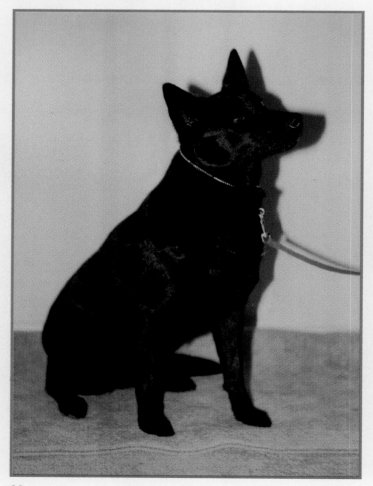

The sit command is easy for your dog to perform and he should master it very quickly.
This Kelpie sits and waits for his next command.

Once your Kelpie learns basic obedience, he can move to advanced levels and possibly competition. Spectre Sarina at a show with Phyllis Sloane.

Call the puppy to you and fuss over him. Place one hand on his hindquarters and the other under his upper chest. Say "Sit" in a pleasant (never harsh) voice. At the same time, push down his rear end and push up under his chest. Now lavish praise on the puppy. Repeat this a few times and your pet will get the idea. Once the puppy is in the sit position you will release your hands. At first he will tend to get up, so immediately repeat the exercise. The lesson will end when the pup is in the sit position. When the puppy understands the command, and does it right away, you can slowly move backwards so that you are a few feet away from him. If he attempts to come to you, simply place him back in the original position and start again. Do not attempt to keep the pup in the sit position for too long. At this age, even a few seconds is a long while and you do not want him to get bored with lessons before he has even begun them.

THE HEEL COMMAND

All dogs should be able to walk nicely on a leash without their owners being involved in a tug-of-war. The heel command will follow leash training. Heel training is best done where you have a wall to one side of you. This will restrict the puppy's lateral movements, so you only have to contend with forward and backward situations. A fence is an alternative, or you can do the lesson in the garage. Again, it is better to do the lesson in private, not on a public sidewalk where there will be many distractions.

With a puppy, there will be no need to use a choke collar as you can be just as effective with a regular

61

one. The leash should be of good length, certainly not too short. You can adjust the space between you, the puppy, and the wall so your pet has only a small amount of room to move sideways. This being so, he will either hang back or pull ahead—the latter is the more desirable state as it indicates a bold pup who is not frightened of you.

Hold the leash in your right hand and pass it through your left. As the puppy moves ahead and strains on the leash, give the leash a quick jerk backwards with your left hand, at the same time saying "Heel." The position you want the pup to be in is such that his chest is level with, or just behind, an imaginary line from your knee. When the puppy is in this position, praise him and

When used correctly, a choke collar can be helpful in teaching your Kelpie to heel. If the dog starts to pull away from you, a quick, gentle tug will get him back into position.

begin walking again, and the whole exercise will be repeated. Once the puppy begins to get the message, you can use your left hand to pat the side of your knee so the pup is encouraged to keep close to your side.

It is useful to suddenly do an about-turn when the pup understands the basics. The puppy will now be behind you, so you can pat your knee and say "Heel." As soon as the pup is in the correct position, give him lots of praise. The puppy will now be beginning to associate certain words with certain actions. Whenever he is not in the heel position he will experience displeasure as you jerk the leash, but when he comes alongside you he will receive praise. Given these two options, he will always prefer the latter—assuming he has no other reason to fear you, which would then create a dilemma in his mind.

Once the lesson has been well learned, then you can adjust your pace from a slow walk to a quick one and the puppy will come to adjust. The slow walk is always the more difficult for most puppies, as they are usually anxious to be on the move.

If you have no wall to walk against then things will be a little more difficult because the pup will tend to wander to his left. This means you need to give lateral jerks as well as bring the pup to your side. End the lesson when the pup is walking nicely beside you. Begin the lesson with a few sit commands (which he understands by now), so you're starting with success and praise. If your puppy is nervous on the leash, you should never drag him to your side as you may see so many other people do (who obviously didn't invest in a good book like you did!). If the pup sits down, call him to your side and give lots of praise. The pup must always come to you because he wants to. If he is dragged to your side he will see you doing the dragging—a big negative. When he races ahead he does not see you jerk the leash, so all he knows is that something restricted his movement and, once he was

Whether sheep or his human family, the Australian Kelpie protects all his charges under his watchful eye. Ch. Butterbone Keepit Dark, owned by Steve Sloane.

in a given position, you gave him lots of praise. This is using canine psychology to your advantage.

Always try to remember that if a dog must be disciplined, then try not to let him associate the discipline with you. This is not possible in all matters but, where it is, this is definitely to be preferred.

THE STAY COMMAND

This command follows from the sit. Face the puppy and say "Sit." Now step backwards, and as you do, say "Stay." Let the pup remain in the position for only a few seconds before calling him to you and giving lots of praise. Repeat this, but step further back. You do not need to shout at the puppy. Your pet is not deaf; in fact, his hearing is far better than yours. Speak just loudly enough for the pup to hear, yet use a firm voice. You can stretch the word to form a "sta-a-a-y." If the pup gets up and comes to you simply lift him up, place him back in the original position, and start again. As the pup comes to understand the command, you can move further and further back.

The next test is to walk away after placing the pup. This will mean your back is to him, which will tempt him to follow you. Keep an eye over your shoulder, and the minute the pup starts to move, spin around and, using a sterner voice, say either "Sit" or "Stay." If the pup has gotten quite close to you, then, again, return him to the original position.

As the weeks go by you can increase the length of time the pup is left in the stay position—but two to three minutes is quite long enough for a puppy. If your puppy drops into a lying position and is clearly more comfortable, there is nothing wrong with this. Likewise, your pup will want to face the direction in which you walked off. Some trainers will insist that the dog faces the direction he was placed in, regardless of whether you move off on his blind side. I have never believed in this sort of obedience because it has no practical benefit.

THE DOWN COMMAND

From the puppy's viewpoint, the down command can be one of the more difficult ones to accept. This is because the position is one taken up by a submissive dog in a wild pack situation. A timid dog will roll over—a natural gesture of submission. A bolder pup will want to get up, and might back off, not feeling he should have to submit to this command. He will feel

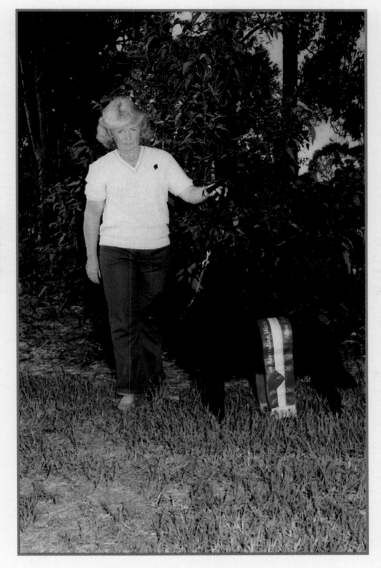

The Australian Kelpie's ability to learn quickly and desire to please his owner make him a top obedience dog and devoted companion.

that he is under attack from you and about to be punished—which is what would be the position in his natural environment. Once he comes to understand this is not the case, he will accept this unnatural position without any problem.

You may notice that some dogs will sit very quickly, but will respond to the down command more slowly— it is their way of saying that they will obey the command, but under protest!

There two ways to teach this command. One is, in my mind, more intimidating than the other, but it is up to you to decide which one works best for you. The first method is to stand in front of your puppy and bring him to the sit position, with his collar and leash on. Pass the leash under your left foot so that when you pull on it, the result is that the pup's neck is forced downwards. With your free left hand, push the pup's shoulders down while at the same time saying "Down." This is when a bold pup will instantly try to back off and wriggle in full protest. Hold the pup firmly by the shoulders so he stays in the position for a second or two, then tell him what a good dog he is and give him lots of praise. Repeat this only a few times in a lesson because otherwise the puppy will get bored and upset over this command. End with an easy command that brings back the pup's confidence.

The second method, and the one I prefer, is done as follows: Stand in front of the pup and then tell him to sit. Now kneel down, which is immediately far less intimidating to the puppy than to have you towering above him. Take each of his front legs and pull them forward, at the same time saying "Down." Release the legs and quickly apply light pressure on the shoulders with your left hand. Then, as quickly, say "Good boy" and give lots of fuss. Repeat two or three times only. The pup will learn over a few lessons. Remember, this is a very submissive act on the pup's behalf, so there is no need to rush matters.

RECALL TO HEEL COMMAND

When your puppy is coming to the heel position from an off-leash situation—such as if he has been running free—he should do this in the correct manner. He should pass behind you and take up his position and then sit. To teach this command, have the pup in front of you in the sit position with his collar and leash on. Hold the leash in your right hand. Give him the command to heel, and pat your left knee. As the pup starts to move forward, use your right hand to guide him behind you. If need be you can hold his collar and walk the dog around the back of you to the desired position. You will need to repeat this a few times until the dog understands what is wanted.

When he has done this a number of times, you can try it without the collar and leash. If the pup comes up toward your left side, then bring him to the sit position in front of you, hold his collar and walk him around the back of you. He will eventually understand and automatically pass around your back each time. If the dog is already behind you when you recall him, then he should automatically come to your left side, which you will be patting with your hand.

THE NO COMMAND

This is a command that must be obeyed every time without fail. There are no halfway stages, he must be 100-percent reliable. Most delinquent dogs have never been taught this command; included in these are the jumpers, the barkers, and the biters. Were your puppy to approach a poisonous snake or any other potential danger, the no command, coupled with the recall, could save his life. You do not need to give a specific lesson for this command because it will crop up time and again in day-to-day life.

If the puppy is chewing a slipper, you should approach the pup, take hold of the slipper, and say "No" in a stern voice. If he jumps onto the furniture, lift him off and say "No" and place him gently on the floor. You must be consistent in the use of the command and apply it every time he is doing something you do not want him to do.

A well-mannered dog is a joy to own. Once you teach your Kelpie the basic commands, you can control your dog in any situation. Spectre Rocket Jason, owned by Steve Sloane.

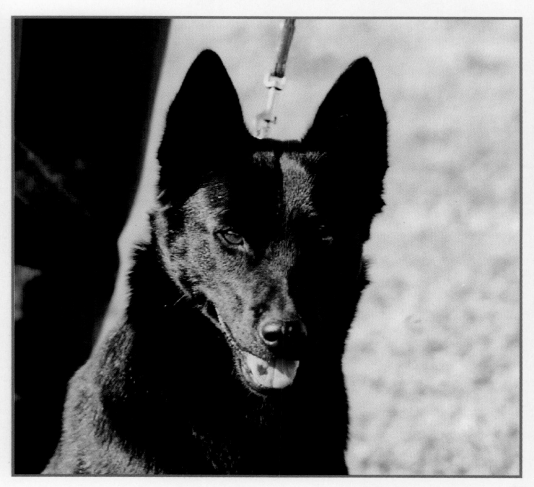

YOUR HEALTHY AUSTRALIAN KELPIE

Dogs, like all other animals, are capable of contracting problems and diseases that, in most cases, are easily avoided by sound husbandry—meaning well-bred and well-cared-for animals are less prone to developing diseases and problems than are carelessly bred and neglected animals. Your knowledge of how to avoid problems is far more valuable than all of the books and advice on how to cure them. Respectively, the only person you should listen to about treatment is your vet. Veterinarians don't have all the answers, but at least they are trained to analyze and treat illnesses, and are aware of the full implications of treatments. This does not mean a few old remedies aren't good standbys when all else fails, but in most cases modern science provides the best treatments for disease.

Opposite: Veterinarians are trained to analyze and treat illnesses. Having complete trust in your chosen veterinarian is tantamount to the long life of your dog.

PHYSICAL EXAMS

Your puppy should receive regular physical examinations or check-ups. These come in two forms. One is obviously performed by your vet, and the other is a day-to-day procedure that should be done by you. Apart from the fact the exam will highlight any problem at an early stage, it is an excellent way of socializing the pup to being handled.

To do the physical exam yourself, start at the head and work your way around the body. You are looking for any sign of lesions, or any indication of parasites on the pup. The most common parasites are fleas and ticks.

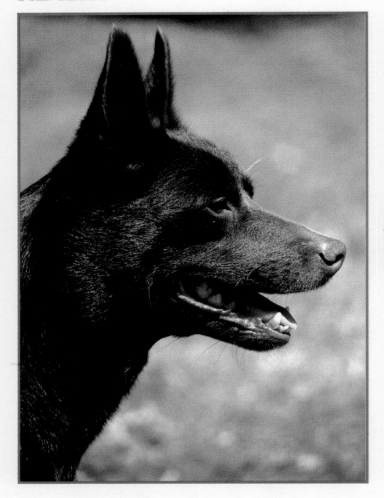

Your veterinarian should perform a thorough oral exam at every check-up to ensure your Kelpie's dental health.

HEALTHY TEETH AND GUMS

Chewing is instinctual. Puppies chew so that their teeth and jaws grow strong and healthy as they develop. As the permanent teeth begin to emerge, it is painful and annoying to the puppy, and puppy owners must recognize that their new charges need something safe upon which to chew. Unfortunately, once the puppy's permanent teeth have emerged and settled solidly into the jaw, the chewing instinct does not fade. Adult dogs instinctively need to clean their teeth, massage their gums, and exercise their jaws through chewing.

It is necessary for your dog to have clean teeth. You should take your dog to the veterinarian at least once a year to have his teeth cleaned and to have his mouth examined for any sign of oral disease. Although dogs do not get cavities in the same way humans do, dogs'

The Hercules® by Nylabone® has raised dental tips that help fight plaque on your Australian Kelpie's teeth and gums.

teeth accumulate tartar, and more quickly than humans do! Veterinarians recommend brushing your dog's teeth daily. But who can find time to brush their dog's teeth daily? The accumulation of tartar and plaque on our dog's teeth when not removed can cause irritation and eventually erode the enamel and finally destroy the teeth. Advanced cases, while destroying the teeth, bring on gingivitis and periodontitis, two very serious conditions that can affect the dog's internal organs as well...to say nothing about bad breath!

Since everyone can't brush their dog's teeth daily or get to the veterinarian often enough for him to scale

Nylafloss® does wonders for your Australian Kelpie's dental health by massaging his gums and literally flossing between his teeth, loosening plaque and tartar build-up. Unlike cotton tug toys, Nylafloss® won't rot or fray.

the dog's teeth, providing the dog with something safe to chew on will help maintain oral hygeine. Chew devices from Nylabone® keep dogs' teeth clean, but they also provide an excellent resource for entertainment and relief of doggie tensions. Nylabone® products give your dog something to do for an hour or two every day and during that hour or two, your dog will be taking an active part in keeping his teeth and gums healthy…without even realizing it! That's invaluable to your dog, and valuable to you!

Nylabone® provides fun bones, challenging bones, and *safe* bones. It is an owner's responsibility to recognize safe chew toys from dangerous ones. Your dog will chew and devour anything you give him. Dogs must not be permitted to chew on items that they can break. Pieces of broken objects can do internal damage to a dog, besides ripping the dog's mouth. Cheap plastic or rubber toys can cause stoppage in the intestines; such stoppages are operable only if caught immediately.

The most obvious choices, in this case, may be the worst choice. Natural beef bones were not designed for chewing and cannot take too much pressure from the sides. Due to the abrasive nature of these bones, they should be offered most sparingly. Knuckle bones, though once very popular for dogs, can be easily

Nylabone® is the only plastic dog bone made of 100% virgin nylon, specially processed to create a tough, durable, completely safe bone.

CHICK-N-CHEEZ CHOOZ™ FROM NYLABONE®

NM-106
REGULAR SIZE
TRIPLE PACK
3 For the price of 2

MADE WITH CHEESE PROTEIN & CHICKEN

NO Added Salt or Sugar
Low in Fat
NO Preservatives

Microwaveable

EDIBLE DIGESTIBLE HEALTH CHEW

Foil Packed For Sealed-in Freshness

Chick-n-Cheez Chooz® are completely safe and nutritious health chews made from pure cheese protein, chicken, and fortified with vitamin E. They contain no salt, sugar, plastic, or preservatives and less than 1% fat.

chewed up and eaten by dogs. At the very least, digestion is interrupted; at worst, the dog can choke or suffer from intestinal blockage.

When a dog chews hard on a Nylabone®, little bristle-like projections appear on the surface of the bone. These help to clean the dog's teeth and add to the gum-massaging. Given the chemistry of the nylon, the bristle can pass through the dog's intestinal tract without effect. Since nylon is inert, no micro-organism can grow on it, and it can be washed in soap and water or sterilized in boiling water or in an auto-clave.

For the sake of your dog, his teeth and your own peace of mind, provide your dog with Nylabones®. They have 100 variations from which to choose.

FIGHTING FLEAS

Fleas are very mobile and may be red, black, or brown in color. The adults suck the blood of the host, while the larvae feed on the feces of the adults, which is rich in blood. Flea "dirt" may be seen on the pup as very tiny clusters of blackish specks that look like freshly ground pepper. The eggs of fleas may be laid on the puppy, though they are more commonly laid off the host in a favorable place, such as the bedding. They normally hatch in 4 to 21 days, depending on the temperature, but they can survive for up to 18 months if temperature conditions are not favorable. The larvae are maggot-like and molt a couple of times before forming pupae, which can survive long periods until the temperature, or the vibration of a nearby host, causes them to emerge and jump on a host.

There are a number of effective treatments available, and you should discuss them with your veterinarian, then follow all instructions for the one you choose. Any treatment will involve a product for your puppy or dog and one for the environment, and will require diligence on your part to treat all areas and thoroughly clean your home and yard until the infestation is eradicated.

THE TROUBLE WITH TICKS

Ticks are arthropods of the spider family, which means they have eight legs (though the larvae have six). They bury their headparts into the host and gorge on its blood. They are easily seen as small grain-like creatures sticking out from the skin. They are often picked up when dogs play in fields, but may also arrive in your yard via wild animals—even birds—or stray cats and dogs. Some ticks are species-specific, others are more adaptable and will host on many species.

The cat flea is the most common flea of dogs. It starts feeding soon after it makes contact with the dog.

The deer tick is the most common carrier of Lyme disease. Photo courtesy of Virbac Laboratories, Inc., Fort Worth, Texas.

The most troublesome type of tick is the deer tick, which spreads the deadly Lyme disease that can cripple a dog (or a person). Deer ticks are tiny and very hard to detect. Often, by the time they're big enough to notice, they've been feeding on the dog for a few days—long enough to do their damage. Lyme disease was named for the area of the United States in which it was first detected—Lyme, Connecticut—but has now been diagnosed in almost all parts of the U.S. Your veterinarian can advise you of the danger to your dog(s) in your area, and may suggest your dog be vaccinated for Lyme. Always go over your dog with a fine-toothed flea comb when you come in from walking through any area that may harbor deer ticks, and if your dog is acting unusually sluggish or sore, seek veterinary advice.

Attempts to pull a tick free will invariably leave the headpart in the pup, where it will die and cause an infected wound or abscess. The best way to remove ticks is to dab a strong saline solution, iodine, or alcohol on them. This will numb them, causing them to loosen their hold, at which time they can be removed with forceps. The wound can then be cleaned and covered with an antiseptic ointment. If ticks are common in your area, consult with your vet for a suitable pesticide to be used in kennels, on bedding, and on the puppy or dog.

INSECTS AND OTHER OUTDOOR DANGERS

There are many biting insects, such as mosquitoes, that can cause discomfort to a puppy. Many diseases are transmitted by the males of these species.

A pup can easily get a grass seed or thorn lodged between his pads or in the folds of his ears. These may go unnoticed until an abscess forms.

This is where your daily check of the puppy or dog will do a world of good. If your puppy has been playing in long grass or places where there may be thorns, pine needles, wild animals, or parasites, the check-up is a wise precaution.

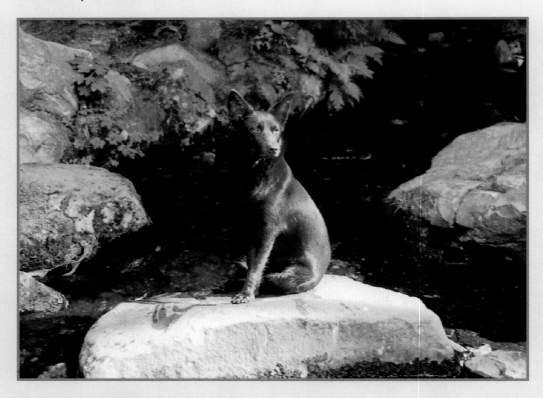

SKIN DISORDERS

Apart from problems associated with lesions created by biting pests, a puppy may fall foul to a number of other skin disorders. Examples are ringworm, mange, and eczema. Ringworm is not caused by a worm, but is a fungal infection. It manifests itself as a sore-looking bald circle. If your puppy should have any form of bald patches, let your veterinarian check him over; a microscopic examination can confirm the condition. Many old remedies for ringworm exist, such as iodine, carbolic acid, formalin, and other tinctures, but modern drugs are superior.

Your Australian Kelpie may encounter fleas or ticks when playing or working outdoors. Be sure to check his coat for any parasites.

Fungal infections can be very difficult to treat, and even more difficult to eradicate, because of the spores. These can withstand most treatments, other than burning, which is the best thing to do with bedding once the condition has been confirmed.

Mange is a general term that can be applied to many skin conditions where the hair falls out and a flaky crust develops and falls away.

Often, dogs will scratch themselves, and this invariably is worse than the original condition, for it opens lesions that are then subject to viral, fungal, or parasitic attack. The cause of the problem can be various species of mites. These either live on skin debris and the hair follicles, which they destroy, or they bury themselves just beneath the skin and feed on the tissue. Applying general remedies from pet stores is not recommended because it is essential to identify the type of mange before a specific treatment is effective.

Eczema is another non-specific term applied to many skin disorders. The condition can be brought about in many ways. Sunburn, chemicals, allergies to foods, drugs, pollens, and even stress can all produce a deterioration of the skin and coat. Given the range of causal factors, treatment can be difficult because the problem is one of identification. It is a case of taking each possibility at a time and trying to correctly diagnose the matter. If the cause is of a dietary nature then you must remove one item at a time in order to find out if the dog is allergic to a given food. It could, of course, be the lack of a nutrient that is the problem, so if the condition persists, you should consult your veterinarian.

INTERNAL DISORDERS

It cannot be overstressed that it is very foolish to attempt to diagnose an internal disorder without the advice of a veterinarian. Take a relatively common problem such as diarrhea. It might be caused by nothing more serious than the puppy hogging a lot of food or eating something that it has never previously eaten. Conversely, it could be the first indication of a potentially fatal disease. It's up to your veterinarian to make the correct diagnosis.

The following symptoms, especially if they accompany each other or are progressively added to earlier symptoms, mean you should visit the veterinarian right away:

Continual vomiting. All dogs vomit from time to time and this is not necessarily a sign of illness. They will eat grass to induce vomiting. It is a natural cleansing process common to many carnivores. However, continued vomiting is a clear sign of a problem. It may be a blockage in the pup's intestinal tract, it may be induced by worms, or it could be due to any number of diseases.

Diarrhea. This, too, may be nothing more than a temporary condition due to many factors. Even a change of home can induce diarrhea, because this often stresses the pup, and invariably there is some change in the diet. If it persists more than 48 hours then something is amiss. If blood is seen in the feces, waste no time at all in taking the dog to the vet.

Running eyes and/or nose. A pup might have a chill and this will cause the eyes and nose to weep. Again, this should quickly clear up if the puppy is placed in a warm environment and away from any drafts. If it does not, and especially if a mucous discharge is seen, then the pup has an illness that must be diagnosed.

Coughing. Prolonged coughing is a sign of a problem, usually of a respiratory nature.

Wheezing. If the pup has difficulty breathing and makes a wheezing sound when breathing, then something is wrong.

Cries when attempting to defecate or urinate. This might only be a minor problem due to the hard state of the feces, but it could be more serious, especially if the pup cries when urinating.

Cries when touched. Obviously, if you do not handle a puppy with care he might yelp. However, if he cries even when lifted gently, then he has an internal problem that becomes apparent when pressure is applied to a given area of the body. Clearly, this must be diagnosed.

Refuses food. Generally, puppies and dogs are greedy creatures when it comes to feeding time. Some might be more fussy, but none should refuse more than one meal. If they go for a number of hours without showing any interest in their food, then something is not as it should be.

General listlessness. All puppies have their off days when they do not seem their usual cheeky, mischievous selves. If this condition persists for more than two days then there is little doubt of a problem. They may not show any of the signs listed, other than perhaps a reduced interest in their food. There are many diseases that can develop internally without displaying obvious clinical signs. Blood, fecal, and other tests are needed in order to identify the disorder before it reaches an advanced state that may not be treatable.

WORMS

There are many species of worms, and a number of these live in the tissues of dogs and most other animals. Many create no problem at all, so you are not even aware they exist. Others can be tolerated in small levels, but become a major problem if they number more than a few. The most common types seen in dogs are roundworms and tapeworms. While roundworms are the greater problem, tapeworms require an intermediate host so are more easily eradicated.

Roundworms are spaghetti-like worms that cause a pot-bellied appearance and dull coat, along with more severe symptoms, such as diarrhea and vomiting. Photo courtesy of Merck AgVet.

Roundworms of the species *Toxocara canis* infest the dog. They may grow to a length of 8 inches (20 cm) and look like strings of spaghetti. The worms feed on the digesting food in the pup's intestines. In chronic cases the puppy will become pot-bellied, have diarrhea, and will vomit. Eventually, he will stop eating, having passed through the stage when he always seems hungry. The worms lay eggs in the puppy and these pass out in his feces. They are then either ingested by the pup, or they are eaten by mice, rats, or beetles. These may then be eaten by the puppy and the life cycle is complete.

Larval worms can migrate to the womb of a pregnant bitch, or to her mammary glands, and this is how they pass to the puppy. The pregnant bitch can be wormed, which will help. The pups can, and should,

Whipworms are hard to find unless you strain your dog's feces, and this is best left to a veterinarian. Pictured here are adult whipworms.

be wormed when they are about two weeks old. Repeat worming every 10 to 14 days and the parasites should be removed. Worms can be extremely dangerous to young puppies, so you should be sure the pup is wormed as a matter of routine.

Tapeworms can be seen as tiny rice-like eggs sticking to the puppy's or dog's anus. They are less destructive, but still undesirable. The eggs are eaten by mice, fleas, rabbits, and other animals that serve as intermediate hosts. They develop into a larval stage and the host must be eaten by the dog in order to complete the chain. Your vet will supply a suitable remedy if tapeworms are seen or suspected. There are other worms, such as hookworms and whipworms, that are also blood suckers. They will make a pup anemic, and blood might be seen in the feces, which can be examined by the vet to confirm their presence. Cleanliness in all matters is the best preventative measure for all worms.

Heartworm infestation in dogs is passed by mosquitoes but can be prevented by a monthly (or daily) treatment that is given orally. Talk to your vet about the risk of heartworm in your area.

BLOAT (GASTRIC DILATATION)

This condition has proved fatal in many dogs, especially large and deep-chested breeds, such as the Weimaraner and the Great Dane. However, any dog can get bloat. It is caused by swallowing air during exercise, food/water gulping or another strenuous task. As many believe, it is not the result of flatulence. The stomach of an affected dog twists, disallowing food and blood flow and resulting in harmful toxins being released into the bloodstream. Death can easily follow if the condition goes undetected.

The best preventative measure is not to feed large meals or exercise your puppy or dog immediately after he has eaten. Veterinarians recommend feeding three smaller meals per day in an elevated feeding rack, adding water to dry food to prevent gulping, and not offering water during mealtimes.

VACCINATIONS

Every puppy, purebred or mixed breed, should be vaccinated against the major canine diseases. These are distemper, leptospirosis, hepatitis, and canine parvovirus. Your puppy may have received a temporary vaccination against distemper before you purchased him, but be sure to ask the breeder to be sure.

The age at which vaccinations are given can vary, but will usually be when the pup is 8 to 12 weeks old. By this time any protection given to the pup by antibodies received from his mother via her initial milk feeds will be losing their strength.

Rely on your veterinarian for the most effectual vaccination schedule for your Australian Kelpie puppy.

The puppy's immune system works on the basis that the white blood cells engulf and render harmless attacking bacteria. However, they must first recognize a potential enemy.

Vaccines are either dead bacteria or they are live, but in very small doses. Either type prompts the pup's defense system to attack them. When a large attack then comes (if it does), the immune system recognizes it and massive numbers of lymphocytes (white blood corpuscles) are mobilized to counter the attack. However, the ability of the cells to recognize these dangerous viruses can diminish over a period of time. It is therefore useful to provide annual reminders about the nature of the enemy. This is done by means of booster injections that keep the immune system on its alert. Immunization is not 100-percent guaranteed to be successful, but is very close. Certainly it is better than giving the puppy no protection.

Dogs are subject to other viral attacks, and if these are of a high-risk factor in your area, then your vet will suggest you have the puppy vaccinated against these as well.

Your puppy or dog should also be vaccinated against the deadly rabies virus. In fact, in many places it is illegal for your dog not to be vaccinated. This is to protect your dog, your family, and the rest of the animal population from this deadly virus that infects the nervous system and causes dementia and death.

ACCIDENTS

All puppies will get their share of bumps and bruises due to the rather energetic way they play. These will usually heal themselves over a few days. Small cuts should be bathed with a suitable disinfectant and then smeared with an antiseptic ointment. If a cut looks more serious, then stem the flow of blood with a towel or makeshift tourniquet and rush the pup to the veterinarian. Never apply so much pressure to the wound that it might restrict the flow of blood to the limb.

In the case of burns you should apply cold water or an ice pack to the surface. If the burn was due to a chemical, then this must be washed away with copious amounts of water. Apply petroleum jelly, or any vegetable oil, to the burn. Trim away the hair if need be. Wrap the dog in a blanket and rush him to the vet. The pup may go into shock, depending on the severity of the burn, and this will result in a lowered blood pressure, which is dangerous and the reason the pup must receive immediate veterinary attention.

It is a good idea to x-ray the chest and abdomen on any dog hit by a car.

If a broken limb is suspected then try to keep the animal as still as possible. Wrap your pup or dog in a blanket to restrict movement and get him to the veterinarian as soon as possible. Do not move the dog's head so it is tilting backward, as this might result in blood entering the lungs.

Do not let your pup jump up and down from heights, as this can cause considerable shock to the joints. Like all youngsters, puppies do not know when enough is enough, so you must do all their thinking for them.

Provided you apply strict hygiene to all aspects of raising your puppy, and you make daily checks on his physical state, you have done as much as you can to safeguard him during his most vulnerable period. Routine visits to your veterinarian are also recommended, especially while the puppy is under one year of age. The vet may notice something that did not seem important to you.

CONGENITAL AND ACQUIRED DISORDERS

by Judy Iby, RVT

Veterinarians and breeders now recognize that many of the disease processes and faults in dogs, as well as in human beings, have a genetic predisposition. These faults are found not only in the purebred dog but in the mixed breed as well. Likely these diseases have been present for decades but more recently are being identified and attributed to inheritance. Fortunately many of these problems are not life threatening or even debilitating. Many of these disorders have a low incidence. It is true that some breeds and some bloodlines within a breed have a higher frequency than others. It is always wise to discuss this subject with breeders of your breed.

Presently very few of the hundreds of disorders can be identified through genetic testing. Hopefully with today's technology and the desire to improve our breeding stock, genetic testing will become more readily available. In the meantime the reputable breeder does the recommended testing for his breed. The American Kennel Club is encouraging OFA (Orthopedic Foundation for Animals) hip and elbow certification and CERF (Canine Eye Registration Foundation) certifications and is listing them on AKC registrations and pedigrees. This is a step forward for the AKC in encouraging better breeding. They also founded a Canine Health Foundation to aid in the research of diseases in the purebred dog.

Opposite: The responsible Kelpie breeder, understanding the potential problems within the breed, strives to produce healthy puppies and contribute to the betterment of the breed.

BONES AND JOINTS

Hip Dysplasia

Canine hip dysplasia has been confirmed in 79 breeds. It is the malformation of the hip joint's ball and socket, with clinical signs from none to severe hip lameness. It may appear as early as five months. The incidence is

Radiograph of a dog with hip dysplasia. Note the flattened femoral head at the marker. Photo courtesy of Toronto Academy of Veterinary Medicine, Toronto, Canada.

reduced within a bloodline by breeding normal to normal, generation after generation. Upon submitting normal pelvic radiographs, the OFA will issue a certification number.

Elbow Dysplasia

Elbow dysplasia results from abnormal development of the ulna, one of the bones of the upper arm. During bone growth, a small area of bone (the anconeal process) fails to fuse with the rest of the bone. This results in an unstable elbow joint and lameness, which is aggravated by exercise. OFA certifies free of this disorder.

Patellar Luxation

This condition can be medial or lateral. Breeders call patellar luxations "slips" for "slipped kneecaps." OFA offers a registry for this disorder. Patellar luxations may or may not cause problems.

Intervertebral Disk Disease (IVD)

IVD is a condition in which a disk(s), the cushion between each vertebrae of the spine, tears and the gel-like material leaks out and presses on the spinal cord. The degeneration is progressive, starting as early as two to nine months, but usually the neurological symptoms are not apparent until three to six years of age. Symptoms include pain, paresis (weariness), incoordination, and paralysis. IVD is a medical emergency. If you are unable to get professional care immediately, then confine your dog to a crate or small area until he can be seen.

Fragmented coronoid process of the elbow, a manifestation of elbow dysplasia. Photo courtesy of Jack Henry.

Spondylitis

Usually seen in middle to old-age dogs and potentially quite serious in the latter, spondylitis is inflammation of the vertebral joints and degeneration of intervertebral disks resulting in bony spur-like outgrowths that may fuse.

CARDIOVASCULAR AND LYMPHATIC SYSTEMS

Dilated Cardiomyopathy

Prevalent in several breeds, this is a disease in which the heart muscle is damaged or destroyed to the point that it cannot pump blood properly through the body resulting in signs of heart failure. Diagnosis is confirmed by cardiac ultrasound.

Lymphosarcoma

This condition can occur in young dogs but usually appears in dogs over the age of five years. Symptoms include fever, weight loss, anorexia, painless enlargement of the lymph nodes, and nonspecific signs of illness. It is the most common type of cancer found in dogs. Chemotherapy treatment will prolong the dog's life but will not cure the disease at this time.

BLOOD

Von Willebrand's Disease

VWD has been confirmed in over 50 breeds and is

a manageable disease. It is characterized by moderate to severe bleeding, corrected by blood transfusions from normal dogs and frequently seen with hypothyroidism. When levels are low, a pre-surgical blood transfusion may be necessary. Many breeders screen their breeding stock for vWD.

Immune-Mediated Blood Disease

Immune-mediated diseases affect the red blood cells and platelets. They are called autoimmune hemolytic anemia or immune-mediated anemia when red blood cells are affected, and autoimmune thrombocytopenic purpura, idiopathic thrombocytopenic purpura, and immune-mediated thrombocytopenia when platelets are involved. The disease may appear acutely. Symptoms include jaundice (yellow color) of the gums and eyes and dark brown or dark red urine. Symptoms of platelet disease include pinpoint bruises or hemorrhages in the skin, gums and eye membranes; nosebleeds; bleeding from the GI tract or into the urine. Any of these symptoms constitutes an emergency!

DIGESTIVE SYSTEM AND ORAL CAVITY

Colitis

This disorder has no known cause and appears with some frequency in certain breeds. It is characterized by an intermittent bloody stool, with or without diarrhea.

Chronic Hepatitis

This is the result of liver failure occuring at relatively young ages. In many cases clinical signs are apparent for less than two weeks. They include anorexia, lethargy, vomiting, depression, diarrhea, trembling or shaking, excess thirst and urination, weight loss, and dark bloody stool. Early diagnosis and treatment promise the best chance for survival.

Copper Toxicity

Copper toxicity occurs when excessive copper is concentrated in the liver. In 1995 there was a breakthrough when the DNA marker was identified in one of the afflicted breeds. Therefore carriers will be identified in the future.

ENDOCRINE SYSTEM

Hypothyroidism

Over 50 breeds have been diagnosed with hypothyroidism. It is the number-one endocrine disorder in the dog and is the result of an underactive thyroid gland. Conscientious breeders are screening their dogs if the disease is common to their breed or bloodline. The critical years for the decline of thyroid function are usually between three and eight, although it can appear at an older age. A simple blood test can diagnose or rule out this disorder. It is easily and inexpensively treated by giving thyroid replacement therapy daily. Untreated hypothyroidism can be devastating to your dog.

Addison's Disease

Primary adrenal insufficiency is caused by damage to the adrenal cortex, and secondary adrenocortical insufficiency is the result of insufficient production of the hormone ACTH by the pituitary gland. Symptoms may include depression, anorexia, a weak femoral pulse, vomiting or diarrhea, weakness, dehydration, and occasionally bradycardia.

Cushing's Disease

Hyperadrenocorticism is the over-production of steroid hormone. Dogs on steroid therapy may show Cushing-like symptoms. Some of the symptoms are excess thirst and urination, hair loss, and an enlarged, pendulous, or flaccid abdomen.

EYES

Cataracts

Breeders should screen their breeding stock for this disorder. A cataract is defined as any opacity of the lens or its capsule. It may progress and produce blindness or it may remain small and cause no clinical impairment of vision. Unfortunately some inherited cataracts appear later in life after the dog has already been bred.

Lens Luxation

This condition results when the lens of the eye is not in normal position, and may result in secondary glaucoma.

Glaucoma

Primary glaucoma is caused by increased intraocular pressure due to inadequate aqueous drainage and is not associated with other intraocular diseases. It may initially be in one eye. Secondary glaucoma is caused by increased intraocular pressure brought on by another ocular disease, tumor, or inflammation.

Keratoconjunctivitis Sicca

"Dry eye" (the decrease in production of tears) may be the result of a congenital or inherited deficiency of the aqueous layer, a lack of the proper nervous stimulation of the tearing system, a traumatic incident, or drugs, including topical anesthetics (such as

An immature cataract is evident in this dilated pupil. The central white area and cloudy areas at 4:00, 6:00 and 8:00 represent the cataract. Photo courtesy of Dr. Kerry L. Ketring.

atropine, and antibiotics containing sulfadiazine, phenazopyridine or salicyla-sulfapyridine). There seems to be an increased incidence of "dry eye" after "cherry eye" removal.

Progressive Retinal Atrophy (PRA)

This is the progressive loss of vision, first at night, followed by total blindness. It is inherited in many breeds.

Distichiasis

Distichiasis results from extra rows of eyelashes growing out of the meibomian gland ducts. This condition may cause tearing, but tearing may be the result of some other problem that needs to be investigated.

Entropion

Entropion is the inward rolling of the eyelid, usually lower lid, which can cause inflammation and may need surgical correction.

Ectropion

Ectropion is the outward rolling of the eyelid, usually lower lid, and may need surgical correction.

Hypertrophy of the Nictitans Gland

"Cherry eye" is the increase in size of the gland resulting in eversion of the third eyelid and is usually bilateral. Onset frequently occurs during stressful periods such as teething.

NEUROMUSCULAR SYSTEM

Epilepsy

Epilepsy is a disorder in which the electrical brain activity "short circuits," resulting in a seizure. Numerous breeds and mixed breeds are subject to idiopathic epilepsy (no explainable reason). Seizures usually begin between six months and five years of age. Don't panic. Your primary concern should be to keep your dog from hurting himself by falling down the stairs or falling off furniture and/or banging his head. Dogs don't swallow their tongues. If the seizure lasts longer than ten minutes, you should contact your veterinarian. Seizures can be caused by many conditions, such as poisoning and birth injuries, brain infections, trauma or tumors, liver disease, distemper, and low blood sugar or calcium. There are all types of seizures from generalized (the dog will be shaking and paddling/kicking his feet) to standing and staring out in space, etc.

UROGENITAL

Cryptorchidism

This is a condition in which either one or both of the testes fail to descend into the scrotum. There should not be a problem if the dog is neutered early, before two to three years of age. Otherwise, the undescended testicle could turn cancerous.

PET OWNERS & BLOOD PRESSURE

Over the past few years, several scientific studies have documented many health benefits of having pets in our lives. At the State University of New York at Buffalo, for example, Dr. Karen Allen and her colleagues have focused on how physical reactions to psychological stress are influenced by the presence of pets. One such study compared the effect of pets with that of a person's close friend and reported pets to be dramatically better than friends at providing unconditional support. Blood pressure was monitored throughout the study, and, on average, the blood pressure of people under stress who were *with* their pets was 112/75, as compared to 140/95 when they were with the self-selected friends. Heart rate differences were also significantly lower when participants were with their pets. A follow-up study included married couples and looked at the stress-reducing effect of pets versus *spouses*, and found, once again, that pets were dramatically more successful than other people in reducing cardiovascular reactions to stress. An interesting discovery made in this study was that when the spouse and pet were *both* present, heart rate and blood pressure came down dramatically.

Other work by the same researchers has looked at the role of pets in moderating age-related increases in blood pressure. In a study that followed 100 women (half in their 20s and half in their 70s) over six months, it was found that elderly women with few social contacts and *no* pets had blood pressures that were significantly higher (averages of 145/95 compared to 120/80) than elderly women with their beloved pets but few *human* contacts. In other words, elderly women with pets, but no friends, had blood pressures that closely reflected the blood pressures of young women.

This series of studies demonstrates that pets can play an important role in how we handle everyday stress, and shows that biological aging cannot be fully understood without a consideration of the social factors in our lives.

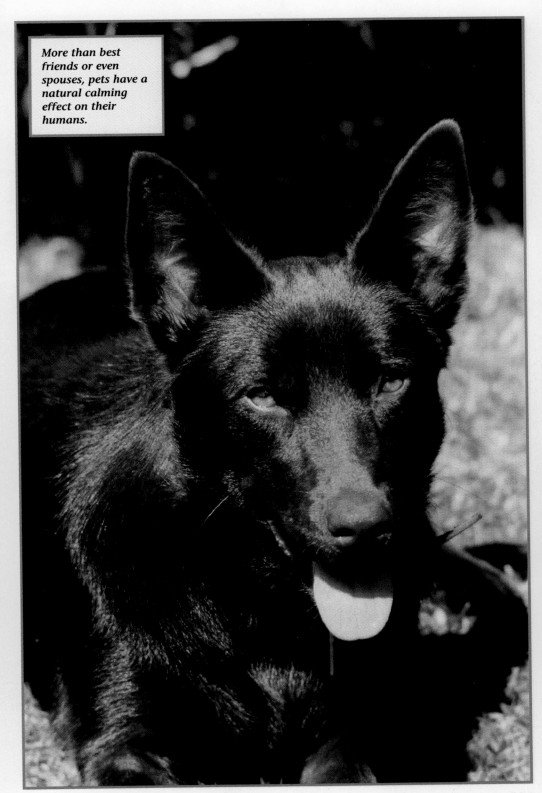

More than best friends or even spouses, pets have a natural calming effect on their humans.

SKULL — Slightly rounded, broad between ears.

STOP
Pronounced.

WITHERS

MUZZLE
Slightly
shorter in
length than
skull.

LIP
Tight,
clean and
free from
looseness.

RUFF

SHOULDER
Clean, muscular and
well sloping.

ELBOW
Neither in
nor out.

FORELEGS
Strong but refined
bone, straight and
parallel.

PASTERN

*Inghall's Blue Exellenth owned by Tuula
Nampajärvi.*